MISSING AND EXPLOITED CHILDREN: HOW TO PROTECT YOUR CHILD

by
Margaret C. Jasper

Oceana's Legal Almanac Series:
Law for the Layperson

Oceana Publications

Information contained in this work has been obtained by Oceana Publications from sources believed to be reliable. However, neither the Publisher nor its authors guarantee the accuracy or completeness of any information published herein, and neither the Publisher nor its authors shall be responsible for any errors, omissions or damages arising from the use of this information. This work is published with the understanding that the Publisher and its authors are supplying information, but are not attempting to render legal or other professional services. If such services are required, the assistance of an appropriate professional should be sought.

Library of Congress Control Number: 2006922579

ISBN 0-19-532157-X
ISBN 978-0-19-532157-9

Oceana's Legal Almanac Series: Law for the Layperson
ISSN 1075-7376

©2006 Oxford University Press, Inc.

Manufactured in the United States of America on acid-free paper.

To My Husband Chris

Your love and support

are my motivation and inspiration

-and-

In memory of my son, Jimmy

Table of Contents

CHAPTER 7:
SEXUAL EXPLOITATION OF CHILDREN

CHAPTER 8:
POST-ABDUCTION STRATEGIES AND RESOURCES

ABOUT THE AUTHOR

MARGARET C. JASPER is an attorney engaged in the general practice of law in South Salem, New York, concentrating in the areas of personal injury and entertainment law. Ms. Jasper holds a Juris Doctor degree from Pace University School of Law, White Plains, New York, is a member of the New York and Connecticut bars, and is certified to practice before the United States District Courts for the Southern and Eastern Districts of New York, the United States Court of Appeals for the Second Circuit, and the United States Supreme Court.

Ms. Jasper has been appointed to the law guardian panel for the Family Court of the State of New York, is a member of a number of professional organizations and associations, and is a New York State licensed real estate broker operating as Jasper Real Estate, in South Salem, New York.

In 2004, Ms. Jasper successfully argued a case before the New York Court of Appeals, which gives mothers of babies who are stillborn due to medical negligence the right to bring a legal action and recover emotional distress damages. This successful appeal overturned a 26-year old New York case precedent, which previously prevented mothers of stillborn babies to sue their negligent medical providers.

Margaret Jasper maintains a website at http://www.JasperLawOffice.com.

Ms. Jasper is the author and general editor of the following legal almanacs:

AIDS Law
The Americans with Disabilities Act
Animal Rights Law
Auto Leasing
Bankruptcy Law for the Individual Debtor
Banks and their Customers
Becoming a Citizen
Buying and Selling Your Home

Commercial Law
Consumer Rights Law
Co-ops and Condominiums: Your Rights and Obligations As Owner
Copyright Law
Credit Cards and the Law
Custodial Rights
Dictionary of Selected Legal Terms
Drunk Driving Law
DWI, DUI and the Law
Education Law
Elder Law
Employee Rights in the Workplace
Employment Discrimination Under Title VII
Environmental Law
Estate Planning
Everyday Legal Forms
Executors and Personal Representatives: Rights and Responsibilities
Harassment in the Workplace
Health Care and Your Rights
Hiring Household Help and Contractors: Your Rights and Obligations Under the Law
Home Mortgage Law Primer
Hospital Liability Law
How To Change Your Name
How To Protect Your Challenged Child
How To Start Your Own Business
Identity Theft and How To Protect Yourself
Individual Bankruptcy and Restructuring
Injured on the Job: Employee Rights, Worker's Compensation and Disability Insurance Law
International Adoption
Juvenile Justice and Children's Law
Labor Law
Landlord-Tenant Law
Law for the Small Business Owner
The Law of Attachment and Garnishment
The Law of Buying and Selling
The Law of Capital Punishment
The Law of Child Custody
The Law of Contracts
The Law of Debt Collection
The Law of Dispute Resolution
The Law of Immigration
The Law of Libel and Slander

The Law of Medical Malpractice
The Law of No-Fault Insurance
The Law of Obscenity and Pornography
The Law of Personal Injury
The Law of Premises Liability
The Law of Product Liability
The Law of Speech and the First Amendment
The Law of Violence Against Women
Lemon Laws
Living Together: Practical Legal Issues
Marriage and Divorce
Missing and Exploited Children: How to Protect Your Child
Motor Vehicle Law
Nursing Home Negligence
Patent Law
Prescription Drugs
Privacy and the Internet: Your Rights and Expectations Under
the Law
Probate Law
Real Estate Law for the Homeowner and Broker
Religion and the Law
Retirement Planning
The Right to Die
Rights of Single Parents
Small Claims Court
Social Security Law
Special Education Law
Teenagers and Substance Abuse
Trademark Law
Victim's Rights Law
Welfare: Your Rights and the Law
What if It Happened to You: Violent Crimes and Victims' Rights
What if the Product Doesn't Work: Warranties & Guarantees
Workers' Compensation Law
Your Child's Legal Rights: An Overview
Your Rights in a Class Action Suit
Your Rights Under the Family and Medical Leave Act
You've Been Fired: Your Rights and Remedies

INTRODUCTION

According to the National Crime Information Center at the U.S. Department of Justice, nearly 2,200 children are reported missing every day. This almanac discusses the topic of missing children and the steps parents can take to ensure the safety of their children.

The almanac presents an overview of the problem and explores the various statutes that have been enacted, and programs that have been established to protect and rescue children from predators, such as sex offender registration under the Jacob Wetterling Act; community notification under Megan's Law; the Amber Alert; and the Code Adam program.

This almanac also discusses parental abduction and the statutes that have been enacted to prevent parental kidnapping and forum shopping in disputed custody cases. International abduction is also examined, including the warning signs and precautions one must take to prevent such an abduction.

This almanac also provides online safety tips and ways to reduce the risks associated with using the Internet, as well as the statutes enacted to protect children while they are online. The sexual exploitation of children is also examined. This almanac also sets forth an action plan for parents whose children are missing.

The Appendix provides applicable statutes, resource directories, and other pertinent information and data. The Glossary contains definitions of many of the terms used throughout the almanac.

CHAPTER 1:
CHILD ABDUCTION: AN OVERVIEW

NATIONAL MISSING CHILDREN'S DAY

On May 25, 1979, 6-year old Etan Patz left his home to catch the school bus. Somewhere between home and the two blocks where his school bus waited, Etan disappeared and was never found. In memory of Etan and all missing children, May 25th—the anniversary of Etan's disappearance—was designated National Missing Children's Day by Presidential Proclamation in 1983. Every U.S. president since that time has continued to proclaim May 25th as National Missing Children's Day, a day devoted to raising awareness about this serious problem.

On National Missing Children's Day 2006, the U.S. Postal Service unveiled it's new "Amber Alert" stamp, which depicts a mother and child in an embrace, and which states "Amber Alert saves missing children." The stamp was created to honor the Amber Alert, a program dedicated to the rapid recovery of abducted children by notifying the surrounding communities of an abduction.

The Amber Alert program is discussed more fully in Chapter 3 of this almanac.

A table of state missing children statutes is set forth at Appendix 1.

ABDUCTION STATISTICS

Every parent worries about the safety of their children, and according to the studies, their fears and concerns are justified. Statistics demonstrate that one child is abducted every 40 seconds in the United States. According to the FBI's National Crime Information Center (NCIC), the number of missing persons reported to law enforcement has increased from 154, 341 in 1982 to 876,213 in 2000, an increase of 468%. Of this total, 85% to 90% were juveniles, and 152,265 abductions were categorized as either endangered or involuntary.

When you hear the term "missing child," it often evokes horrific images of abduction and abuse by a stranger, however, a child can be missing for a number of reasons other than stranger abduction. The largest number of missing children are runaways, followed by family abductions, and lost, injured, or otherwise missing children; while the smallest number of missing children are victims of non-family abductions, which is the most dangerous type of abduction.

Based on the identity of the perpetrator, there are three distinct types of abduction: (i) abduction by a relative of the victim or "family abduction" (49%), (ii) kidnapping by an acquaintance of the victim or "acquaintance abduction" (27%); and (iii) kidnapping by a stranger of the victim or "stranger abduction" (24%). Both acquaintance abduction and stranger abduction are generally referred to as "non-family abduction."

Family Abduction

Family abduction is committed primarily by parents, usually originates in the home, and involves a larger percentage of female perpetrators (43%) than other types of kidnapping offenses. Family abduction occurs more frequently with children under the age of 6, and both boys and girls are equally victimized. Most family abductions occur in the context of custody disputes.

Parental abduction is discussed more fully in Chapter 5 of this almanac.

Non-Family Abduction

A non-family abduction involves an abductor who is unrelated to the child. Statistics indicate that the identity of the perpetrator in a non-family abduction is just as likely to be someone known to the child or family as it is to be a stranger. Non-family abductions can be broken down as follows:

1. Friend (17%)
2. Acquaintance (21%)
3. Neighbor (5%)
4. Caretaker (4%)
5. Stranger (45%)
6. Other (8%)

Acquaintance Abduction

Acquaintance abduction has the largest percentage of female and teenage victims, and is more often associated with other crimes, such as sexual and physical assault. Acquaintance abduction often occurs in homes and residences, and has the highest percentage of injured victims.

Stranger Abduction

Stranger abduction occurs primarily outdoors. Stranger abduction is the most dangerous type of kidnapping, and most often involves the use of a firearm. Although studies indicate that the murder of a child abducted by a stranger is a rare event, when it does occur, 75% of those children who are murdered are dead within three hours of being abducted.

All of our children are at risk of stranger abduction regardless of their _____ fact, even though parents tend to be _____ the younger child, according to the _____ e older child that is most vulnerable,

_____ of Justice, more females than males _____ g:

_____ s most often associated with the sex- _____ e robbery of a boy victim.

_____ istance Act of 1984, the Office of Juve- _____ vention (OJJDP) is required to conduct _____ number of children reported missing ven year. There have been two studies _____ requirement: NISMART-1 (1988) and _____ is an acronym for "National Incidence _____ naway and Thrownaway Children."

_____ ompared to the data from NISMART-2 _____ ies of children comprise the study: (i) victims of family abductions; (ii) runaways; and (iii) thrownaways, lost, injured, or otherwise missing children.

Victims of Family Abductions

For purposes of the study, a "broad scope" family abduction occurs if, in violation of a custody agreement or decree, a family member took a child or failed to return a child at the end of a legal or agreed-upon visit, and the child was kept at least overnight. A subcategory, termed a "policy focal" family abduction, includes one of three additional conditions: (1) the abductor attempted to conceal the taking or whereabouts of the child, or prevent contact with the child; (2) the abductor transported the child out of state; or (3) evidence exists that the abductor intended to keep the child indefinitely or to affect custodial privileges permanently.

The study found that the incidence rate for children who experienced broad scope family abductions declined significantly from 5.62 per 1,000 children in 1988 to 4.18 per 1,000 children in 1999. There was a statistically insignificant increase in the incidence rate for children who experienced "policy focal" family abductions from 2.59 per 1,000 children in 1988 to 3.15 per 1,000 children in 1999.

Runaways

For purposes of the study, a "broad scope" runaway is an episode that meets one of the following criteria: (1) a child left home without permission and was away at least one night; (2) a child made a statement or left a note indicating intent to run away and then stayed away at least overnight; (3) a child age 15 or older who was away, chose not to come home when expected, and stayed away at least two nights; or (4) a child age 14 or younger who was away, chose not to come home when expected, and stayed away at least one night. A "policy focal" runaway episode requires the additional condition that the child was without a familiar and secure place to stay for at least one night.

The study found that the incidence rate for broad scope runaways declined from 7.09 per 1,000 children in 1988 to 5.28 per 1,000 children in 1999. There was a statistically insignificant decrease in the incidence rate for policy focal runaways from 2.06 per 1,000 children in 1988 to 1.26 per 1,000 children in 1999.

Thrownaways

For purposes of the study, "thrownaway" children are those children whose parent or caretaker asked them to leave the home. The study was unable to obtain an accurate measure of thrownaway children, possibly due to the fact that those households participating in the study may have been reluctant to admit having forced their children out of the home.

Lost/Injured/Otherwise Missing Children

For purposes of the study, a "broad scope" lost, injured, or otherwise missing child episode meets one of the following criteria:

(1) a child disappeared from home or from parental supervision and could not be located for varying amounts of time depending on age:

(i) any amount of time for a child age 0–2

(ii) 2 hours for a child age 3–4

(iii) 3 hours for a child age 5–6

(iv) 4 hours for a child age 7–10

(v) 8 hours for a child age 11–13

(vi) overnight for a child age 14–17

(vii) 1 hour for a child of any age with a serious or permanent physical or mental disability or impairment or life threatening medical condition; or

(2) a child who was out with parental permission failed to return, could not be located, and was gone at least overnight; or

(3) a child who was out with parental permission failed to return or make contact with the parent for at least an hour after return or contact was expected because the child suffered harm or an injury that required medical attention.

A "policy focal" lost, injured, or otherwise missing episode requires the additional condition that the police were contacted to help locate the child.

The study found that the incidence rate for children who experienced broad scope lost, injured, or otherwise missing episodes decreased significantly, from 6.95 per 1,000 children in 1988 to 3.40 per 1,000 children in 1999. The incidence rate for children who experienced policy focal lost, injured, or otherwise missing episodes declined from 2.21 per 1,000 children in 1988 to 0.51 per 1,000 children in 1999.

ABDUCTION PREVENTION MEASURES

Talk to Your Child About Safety Issues

There is no "right age" to start teaching your child how to protect themselves. However, the manner in which you teach your child about personal safety depends largely on the child's ability to understand the safety measures and put them into practice. Therefore, when giving your child safety tips, consider his or her age and developmental level.

Safety at Home

With the younger child, you should practice safety skills repeatedly until it becomes second nature to them. Make sure your child knows his or her name, phone number, and address. Provide them with a card containing this information, as well as any other contact numbers, such as your business number, cell phone number, emergency contact number, etc. In addition, post the contact information in the home, e.g., on a kitchen bulletin board. Children should know whom to call in case of an emergency, such as a relative or close adult family friend. Children should also know how to dial "911" in case of an emergency.

If your child is mature enough to come home after school when there is nobody else at home, tell him or her to make sure that nobody has followed them home, and to lock the doors when they get inside. It is also a good idea to maintain telephone contact with your child while they are home alone. Instruct your child not to let any callers or visitors know that they are home alone without adult supervision. For example, if your child answers the phone and the caller asks to speak with you, your child should simply say that you are busy, and not divulge that you are not home.

If you need to hire a babysitter to care for your child, e.g., while you are at work, make sure you thoroughly check out the babysitter's references. It is also a good idea to go home at a time when the babysitter isn't expecting you so you can see for yourself how the children are being cared for in your absence. Also, regularly ask your children how their day went and listen carefully for any "red flags" that may alert you to a problem.

Safety at Play

Know where your child is at all times when they go out to play. Define their boundaries and make sure they understand where they can and cannot travel. Make a list of acceptable places they can go, such as the town park, the school playground, etc. Teach them the buddy system. They shouldn't venture around the neighborhood alone. Child predators routinely drive through neighbourhoods looking for their next victim. For example, as discussed in Chapter 3 of this almanac, 9-year-old Amber Hagerman ("Amber Alert") was riding her bicycle near her home when a man pulled her off her bicycle and threw her into the front seat of his pickup truck.

Know your neighbors, and let your child know which neighbors they should go to in case of an emergency if you are not available. Routinely check out your state's sex offender registration website to find out whether any potentially dangerous child predators have moved into—or in close proximity to—your neighborhood. Many families are unaware that dangerous convicted sex offenders are living in their midst. For example, as discussed in Chapter 2 of this almanac, 7-year old Megan Kanka ("Megan's Law) accepted an invitation into the home of a neighbor to see his new puppy, where she was raped and murdered. Unknown to the community, that neighbor was a twice-convicted pedophile.

Sex offender registration is discussed more fully in Chapter 2 of this almanac.

Do not drop your children off alone at the movie theatre, video arcade, shopping mall, park, or swimming pool, etc. Child predators know the places children like to visit, and often hang around these areas waiting for their next victim. For example, as discussed in Chapter 4 of this almanac, 6-year old Adam Walsh ("Code Adam") was playing video games in a department store along with other children when he was abducted.

Make sure your child knows not to speak to any strange adult, and explain all of the possible tricks an adult may use to lure them, such as:

"Your parent was injured and sent me to bring you home"

"I lost my puppy, can you help me find it?"

"Would you like some candy?"

If a stranger approaches or puts their hand on your child, instruct him or her to scream as loud as possible to gain attention. Child predators do not want to create a scene. If there is nobody around, tell your child to fight back as hard as possible. Once the abductor gets your child in their car, it is difficult to escape. If your child does end up in the stranger's car, he or she should do everything possible to bring attention to the vehicle. Experts have said, if all else fails, grab hold of the steering wheel and try to steer the car into a tree or some other obstacle. Once the child predator reaches their destination, the likelihood of serious harm to your child increases. A child predator will tell the child that if he or she cooperates, everything will be fine. This is absolutely untrue and your child should be told never to trust the abductor—escape at all costs.

Go over all the possible scenarios and tell your child exactly what he or she must do in every situation. Tell them never to get into a stranger's car, no matter what they are told. Children—particularly young children—may get worried when they hear you've been injured, or excited by the lure of a new puppy or candy. That is why you have to regularly repeat these warnings to your children over and over until they are able to instinctively recognize a potentially dangerous situation.

CHILD IDENTIFICATION KITS

As stated above, statistically, it is unlikely your child will ever end up missing, however, you should still take precautionary measures. It is a good idea to put together a child identification kit, particularly for a young child whose appearance may change significantly over short periods of time. Your child identification kit should contain:

1. A complete description of your child, including hair and eye color; height and weight; any distinguishing characteristics, e.g., eyeglasses, birth marks, etc. Update the description regularly.

2. Color photographs of your child. (Make sure the photographs clearly depict your child's face. Take new photographs at least every six months.)

3. Copies of your child's medical records.

4. Your child's fingerprint card.

5. Your child's DNA sample.

Do-It-Yourself DNA Sample Kit

In 1993, Polly Klass was 12-years old when she was kidnapped at knifepoint by a violent ex-convict during a slumber party in her own home in Petaluma, California. Polly's body was found two months later. She had been strangled. The non-profit KlassKids Foundation was established in Polly's memory, one year after her abduction. The mission of the KlassKids Foundation is to stop crimes against children.

As part of their mission, the KlaasKids Foundation and the State of California DNA Laboratory created a Do-It-Yourself DNA Collection Kit using common household items. DNA is becoming the new "genetic fingerprint" that has become invaluable in making a proper identification. Following are the steps necessary to sample and save your child's DNA:

1. Rub a clean, sterile cotton swab on the inside of your child's cheek until it is moist.

2. Let the cotton swab air dry for 24 hours.

3. When it is dry, place the cotton swab in a zip-lock bag and seal the bag.

4. With a permanent pen, label the bag with your child's name and the date you took the DNA sample.

5. Place the bag inside a second zip-lock bag and save it in your freezer in case the DNA sample is ever needed.

EXPECTANT PARENTS

Every so often there is a news report about an infant abducted from the hospital after birth. Although this type of abduction is rare, and health care facilities are taking extra precautions to avoid kidnappings and mix-ups in the hospital setting, expectant parents should also be aware of certain infant abduction prevention measures.

Expectant parents should inquire about the safety protocol in the maternity ward of the hospital where the birth will take place, and ask for a copy of any written security procedures, if possible. Ask about visitation policies, e.g., the hours, who is permitted to visit, etc.

It is now customary for newborns to be out of the nursery and left in the room with their mother for extended periods of time during the day. Never leave your infant unattended. If you need to use the restroom, and there is no family member in the room, summon a nurse to the room to attend your baby. If you need to take a nap, ask the nurse to take your baby back to the nursery while you are sleeping. However, do not give your newborn to any person you do not know, or who does not have proper identification, even if they are in hospital attire. You could be unwittingly handing your baby over to an abductor.

During your hospital stay, many people will enter and exit your room for a variety of reasons, e.g., doctors, nurses, attendants, social workers, and other hospital employees. You should familiarize yourself with the maternity ward staff and, if an unfamiliar individual enters your room, you have a right to know who that person is, their purpose for being there, and request identification. If a hospital employee comes in to your room to transport your newborn for tests, again, do not let your baby leave until you identify the individual and are satisfied that they have a legitimate reason for handling your child.

Before you are discharged, make sure you have a file containing your newborn's footprints, color photographs of your infant, and the baby's physical description, e.g., length, width, and any special characteristics, e.g, a birthmark, etc. Once you are discharged, do not allow strangers or recent acquaintances in your home. If your hospital arranges for follow-up newborn healthcare visits in your home, make sure you request identification before allowing anyone access to your baby. Make sure you vigilantly watch your newborn when out in public. Do not let strangers hold your infant, even for a moment. Unfortunately, there are abductors who target newborns, oftentimes as part of a baby-selling scam.

CHAPTER 2:
SEX OFFENDER REGISTRATION AND COMMUNITY NOTIFICATION

IN GENERAL

As of July 1, 2005, there were 563,806 registered sex offenders in the United States. Studies show that sex offenders pose a high risk of repeat behavior following their conviction or release from prison. Thus, it was recognized that there was a need for legislation to protect the public, especially children, from these sexual predators.

A table of registered sex offenders as of July 1, 2005, by state, is set forth at Appendix 2.

THE JACOB WETTERLING ACT—SEX OFFENDER REGISTRATION

In 1989, 11-year old Jacob Wetterling, his 10-year old brother, Trevor, and their 11-year old friend, were riding their bikes while returning home from a convenience store in St. Joseph, Minnesota. A masked man came out of a driveway and ordered the boys to throw their bikes into a ditch, turn off their flashlights, and lie face down on the ground. The gunman asked each of the boys his age. Upon hearing their ages, he told Trevor and Aaron to run away or he would shoot them. As they ran away, they looked back to see the gunman grab Jacob's arm. Jacob has never been found.

Friends and strangers worked around the clock to search for Jacob. Flyers were distributed throughout the country. It was subsequently discovered that, unknown to local law enforcement, halfway houses in the St. Joseph area housed sex offenders after their release from prison.

Following Jacob's tragic abduction, his mother, Patty, became an advocate for missing children and was appointed to a Governor's Task Force that recommended stronger sex offender registration requirements in

Minnesota. In 1994, recognizing the seriousness of the problem, Congress passed the Jacob Wetterling Crimes Against Children and Sexually Violent Offender Act in memory of Jacob.

The Jacob Wetterling Act is set forth at Appendix 3.

Under the Act, all states were required to implement a sex-offender registration program. Congress used the "carrot and stick" approach to ensure compliance with the law. States that failed to establish a sex offender registration program were subject to a ten percent forfeiture of federal funds for state and local law enforcement. As a result, all fifty states implemented a sex offender registry.

Under the law, individuals convicted of sexually related crimes are required to register as sex offenders with the state after conviction, or if they serve time in prison, upon their release. Offenders must also notify the state's registry when they relocate. Prior to their release from prison, jail, a mental hospital, or while on probation, sex offenders are generally notified in writing of their duty to register, and a copy of the notification letter is forwarded to the appropriate law enforcement agency.

In general, registered sex offenders are also required to update their information at set times. In some cases, certain sex offenders—e.g., transients and sexually violent predators—must update their information more frequently than other sex offenders. For example, if a registrant changes his or her address, they are required to update their registration information within a specified number of days.

The states track the dates of the sex offender's required updates and, if a registered sex offender fails to update their information by the deadline, they are in violation of the law.

Privacy Rights

Opponents of the sex offender registration laws argue that the registration requirement impinges on the privacy rights of those individuals who have "paid their debt to society" by serving their prison sentence. However, it was found that the sex offender registration laws were constitutional because the government's interest in protecting the public from sex offenders is paramount to the privacy rights of those individuals convicted of sex offenses. This was due, in large part, to the high recidivism rate of sex offenders, the nature of their crimes, and the vulnerability of the innocent children who are the sex offender's largest target group.

MEGAN'S LAW—COMMUNITY NOTIFICATION

In 1994, 7-year old Megan Kanka accepted an invitation from a neighbor in Hamilton Township, New Jersey, to see his new puppy. Unknown to the community, the neighbor was a twice-convicted pedophile. He raped Megan, murdered her, and dumped her body in a nearby park.

Following this tragedy, there was outrage over Megan's tragic and unnecessary murder. Megan's parents said that they would never have allowed her to travel the neighborhood freely if they had known that a convicted sex offender was living across the street. The public demanded to know whether child molesters were also living in their neighborhood. The Kanka family joined in the fight for a community notification law that would warn the public about sex offenders living in their area.

Realizing that the sex offender registration requirement under the Jacob Wetterling Act did not adequately protect the public, particularly the children who are most vulnerable to child sexual predators, legislators responded by passing a federal law mandating state community notification programs. On May 17, 1996, Megan's Law was enacted as an amendment to the Jacob Wetterling Act:

(e) **Release of information**

(1) The information collected under a State registration program may be disclosed for any purpose permitted under the laws of the State.

(2) The State or any agency authorized by the State shall release relevant information that is necessary to protect the public concerning a specific person required to register under this section, except that the identity of a victim of an offense that requires registration under this section shall not be released. The release of information under this paragraph shall include the maintenance of an Internet site containing such information that is available to the public and instructions on the process for correcting information that a person alleges to be erroneous.

(42 U.S.C. § 14071)

Under Megan's Law, all states are required to implement a community notification program and maintain sex offender websites where sex offender information is posted and made accessible to the public. Since the passage of the federal legislation, all states have passed some form of Megan's Law.

Different states have different procedures for making the required disclosures. In general, the statutes set forth three levels of sex offenders: Level 1 (low risk), Level 2 (moderate risk), and Level 3 (high risk). Local law enforcement generally decides whether to notify the public about Level 2 and 3 offenders, however, information about Level 1 offenders is not usually made public.

A directory of state sex offender registration websites is set forth at Appendix 4.

THE PAM LYCHNER SEXUAL OFFENDER TRACKING AND IDENTIFICATION ACT OF 1996

Houston real estate agent Pam Lychner prepared to show a vacant home to a prospective buyer. Awaiting her at the house was a twice-convicted felon who brutally assaulted her. Her husband arrived and saved her life. She then formed "Justice for All," a victims rights advocacy group that lobbies for tougher sentences for violent criminals.

Pam Lychner helped craft the language of a bill that established a national database to track sex offenders. Pam Lychner and her two daughters were killed in the explosion of TWA Flight 800 off the coast of Long Island in July 1996. Later that year, in her memory, Congress enacted the Pam Lychner Sexual Offender Tracking and Identification Act of 1996 as an amendment to the Jacob Wetterling Act. The Act requires lifetime registration for recidivists and offenders who commit certain aggravated offenses.

THE COMMERCE, JUSTICE, AND STATE, THE JUDICIARY, AND RELATED AGENCIES APPROPRIATIONS ACT (CJSA)

In 1998, provisions contained in Section 115 of the General Provisions of Title I of the Commerce, Justice, and State, the Judiciary, and Related Agencies Appropriations Act (CJSA) amended the sex offender registration requirements of the Jacob Wetterling Act. The amendments include:

1. heightened registration requirements for sexually violent offenders;

2. registration of federal and military offenders;

3. registration of nonresident workers and students; and

4. participation in the National Sex Offender Registry (NSOR).

THE CAMPUS SEX CRIMES PREVENTION ACT

In 2000, the Campus Sex Crimes Prevention Act was enacted as an amendment to the Jacob Wetterling Act. The Act requires offenders to report information regarding any enrollment or employment at an institution of higher education and to provide this information to the law enforcement agency whose jurisdiction includes the institution.

CHAPTER 3:
THE AMBER ALERT PROGRAM

HISTORY AND BACKGROUND—THE AMBER HAGERMAN CASE

In January 1996, nine-year-old Amber Hagerman was riding her bicycle near her home in Arlington, Texas, when a neighbor witnessed a man pull Amber off her bicycle, throw her into the front seat of his pickup truck, and drive away at a high speed. The neighbor called police and provided a description of the suspect and his vehicle. The FBI and local police department conducted an investigation and search. Local radio and television stations covered the story in their regular broadcasts. Four days later, Amber's body was found in a drainage ditch four miles from her home. Her throat had been cut. To date, her abductor has not been found.

Following Amber's abduction and murder, a concerned citizen contacted a Dallas area radio station with a suggestion to help prevent similar tragedies. The idea was for Dallas radio stations to broadcast news bulletins about abducted children in the same way they handle severe weather alerts. The plan was presented to the Association of Radio Managers (ARM) and, in July 1997, the Amber Alert program was established in memory of Amber Hagerman. AMBER is also an acronym for America's Missing: Broadcast Emergency Response.

Since that time, the Amber Alert program has been adopted by all 50 states, and has saved the lives of more than 200 children nationwide.

A directory of state Amber Alert contacts is set forth at Appendix 5.

WHAT IS THE AMBER ALERT PROGRAM?

Under the Amber Alert program, when a child's disappearance meets certain criteria, law enforcement officials notify the media. Radio and television stations interrupt their regular programming and, using the Emergency Alert System (EAS), broadcast relevant information concerning the kidnapping to the public. The information includes a de-

---

scription of the child, the suspect, and any vehicle involved in the abduction. The goal is to obtain the immediate assistance of the community in finding the child as quickly as possible insofar as time is of the essence in successfully recovering the child unharmed.

An Amber Alert can be issued across state and jurisdictional lines. Many states have formal memorandums of understanding with other states. A number of other states have informal agreements with other states to issue Amber Alerts upon request. In addition, there are currently 27 regional plans. If law enforcement in one state has reason to believe that the child has been taken across state lines, the Amber Alert state coordinator will ask the second state to issue an alert.

CRITERIA FOR AMBER ALERT ACTIVATION

When law enforcement officials receive notification that a child has been kidnapped, they must first determine whether the abduction meets the recommended activation criteria set forth by the U.S. Department of Justice, as follows:

1. There must be a reasonable belief by law enforcement that an abduction has occurred to avoid abuse of the system. It is also essential to determine the level of risk to the child. For example, stranger abductions are the most dangerous type of abduction and are the program's primary concern.

2. The abduction is of a child age 17 years or younger. The Department of Justice recommends that all states adopt this age standard or, in the alternative, agree to honor the age limit of another state.

3. The law-enforcement agency must believe that the child is in imminent danger of serious bodily injury or death. Again, this element is related to the primary concern over stranger abductions, which represent the greatest danger to children.

4. There must be a enough descriptive information about the victim and the abduction for law enforcement to issue an Amber Alert, insofar as the program is based on the expectation that the public will be on the lookout for the child, thus necessitating a complete and accurate description to be effective.

5. The child's name and the circumstances surrounding the abduction must be entered into the National Crime Information Center (NCIC) computer, and the case must be flagged as a child abduction. Although many state plans do not require data entry into the NCIC database, failure to do so undermines the goal of the Amber Alert program. Entry of the Amber Alert data expands the search for an ab-

ducted child from the local, state, or regional level to the national level.

If the U.S. Department of Justice criteria are met, the information is prepared for public distribution, and faxed to radio stations designated as primary stations under the EAS. The primary stations send the same information to area radio and television stations and cable systems via the EAS, and participating stations immediately broadcast the information to their listeners. Radio stations interrupt programming to announce the Alert, and television stations and cable systems run a "crawl" on the screen along with a picture of the child.

Some states have begun to include electronic billboards in their Amber Alert programs. The electronic billboards have routinely been used to alert drivers about accidents and traffic delays. Now those same billboards are being used to alert drivers about abducted children by displaying a description of the child, the abductor, and/or the vehicle.

RESPONDING TO AN AMBER ALERT

If you are in the area when an Amber Alert is issued, you are encouraged to be on the lookout for the abducted child, the suspected kidnapper, and any vehicle reportedly involved in the abduction. If you see a child, suspect or vehicle that fits the Amber Alert description, immediately call the number provided in the alert, and give law enforcement authorities any information you may have regarding the child, the suspect and/or the vehicle.

THE PROTECT ACT OF 2003

On April 30, 2003, the Prosecutorial Remedies and Other Tools to End the Exploitation of Children Today (PROTECT) Act was signed into law. The PROTECT Act is a comprehensive piece of federal legislation designed to strengthen the ability of law enforcement agencies to prevent, investigate, prosecute and punish violent crimes committed against children. Under the Act, a national Amber Alert program was established, and a national coordinator was appointed, to coordinate state and local Amber Alert programs, and develop guidance for the issuance of Amber Alerts.

Some of the most important provisions of the PROTECT Act are as follows:

1. There is no statute of limitations for crimes involving the abduction or physical or sexual abuse of a child, in virtually all cases. Under previous law, the statute of limitations expired when the child

turned 25, potentially allowing child rapists to go free if law enforcement could not solve the crime in time.

2. The Act makes it more difficult for defendants accused of serious crimes against children to obtain bail.

3. The Act strengthens laws punishing offenders who travel abroad to prey on children—a practice known as "sex tourism."

4. The Act increased penalties for non-family member child abduction.

5. The Act increased penalties for sexual exploitation of children and child pornography, e.g., the sentence for a first offense of using a child to produce child pornography now ranges from 15 to 30 years.

6. The Act contains a "two strikes" provision that requires life imprisonment for offenders who commit two serious sexual abuse offenses against a child.

7. The Act limits the judiciary's authority to give reduced prison sentences based on "downward departure" grounds.

8. The Act eliminates the 5-year cap of post-release supervision of sex offenders and allows supervised release for any term of years, even for life.

9. The Act strengthens the prohibition on "virtual" child pornography, prohibits any obscene materials that depict children, and provides for tougher penalties.

10. The Act encourages greater voluntary reporting of suspected child pornography found by Internet service providers on their systems.

The PROTECT Act of 2003 is set forth at Appendix 6.

THE AMBER ALERT LEGAL DATABASE

The Amber Alert legal database compiles and organizes Amber Alert laws into one primary statutory resource that enables an individual to ascertain the law in his or her own jurisdiction, as well as any requirements imposed by federal or international law.

THE WIRELESS AMBER ALERTS INITIATIVE

The Wireless Amber Alerts Initiative is a voluntary partnership between the wireless industry, law-enforcement agencies, and the National Center for Missing & Exploited Children (NCMEC), to distribute AMBER Alerts to wireless subscribers who are able to receive text messages on their wireless devices, and choose to receive Amber Alert messages.

You can sign up for wireless Amber Alerts at www.wirelessamberalerts. org or by visiting your wireless carrier's website. You will need to provide your wireless phone numbers, including area code, and designate up to five zip codes for which you want to receive wireless Amber Alerts. There is no cost to the subscriber for participating in the wireless alert program.

When an Amber Alert is issued in one of the zip codes you designated, you will receive a text message on your wireless device after one is issued. Sometimes an Amber Alert will be issued statewide or for an entire metropolitan area, which includes one of the zip codes you have chosen. This means that you may receive an alert for an area that is larger than what might be covered by your particular zip code entry.

CHAPTER 4:
CODE ADAM

HISTORY AND BACKGROUND: THE ADAM WALSH CASE

Most parents have experienced the sense of panic when they are out with their child in a public place, and turn their back for a second, only to discover their child is suddenly gone. It only takes a moment for a child to disappear. Sometimes, the child just runs off to play amongst the clothing racks in a department store, or becomes distracted and simply gets lost. However, until your child is found unharmed and is safe by your side again, the terrifying images of your child being kidnapped can be overwhelming.

This nightmare scenario came true for John and Reve Walsh in 1981, when their 6-year old son Adam was abducted from a shopping mall in Florida and murdered. Adam and his mother were shopping for lamps in a department store close to their home when Adam saw some children playing video games in the store. Adam's mother let him play video games while she looked at lamps a short distance away.

In less than 10 minutes, she looked for Adam but he was gone. After two hours of searching, the police were called. Flyers with Adam's photograph were distributed throughout the area, however, sixteen days later, Adam's body was found. The Code Adam program was established in 1994 in Adam's memory. The program is designed to protect innocent children like Adam.

WHAT IS CODE ADAM?

It has been recognized that a swift and effective response is critical for the recovery of an abducted child. According to law enforcement studies, the abducted child has an estimated three-hour life expectancy, and there is typically a two-hour delay before the police are notified that a child is missing. The Code Adam program was designed to help ensure the safe recovery of these abducted children.

The Code Adam program is one of the nation's largest child safety programs with thousands of establishments participating in the effort to safeguard our most vulnerable population. Code Adam is a special alert issued over the public address system of a participating establishment when a customer reports a missing child. The program trains store personnel and other public building authorities in strategies to prevent child abductions and to respond efficiently in cases of suspected child abductions on their premises. Businesses participating in the program post a special decal at the entrance of their establishment to let customers know they take part in the Code Adam program.

The Code Adam program was initially conceived in 1994 by a loss prevention supervisor for Wal-Mart, who read a newspaper article about an attempted abduction at a local shopping mall, and decided to do something about it. His idea was to create a special store code to be used in the event of an abduction or attempted abduction. The safety team leader of a Wal-Mart store came up with the idea of naming it "Code Adam" in memory of Adam Walsh.

CODE ADAM TRAINING

Code Adam participants and their employees, as well as public building authorities, receive training regarding the protocols and procedures in responding to a suspected child abduction. The attendees are instructed on the steps to take when a missing child is reported to them. In addition, the training program provides background information on the incidence of abduction, abductor and victim characteristics, important federal and state laws, resources, and prevention strategies. By undergoing the training program, store and building personnel learn how to swiftly take appropriate action when they receive a missing child report.

CODE ADAM PROCEDURES

When a Code Adam is activated, the establishment's employees are required to follow the procedural steps listed below:

1. If a visitor reports a child missing, the employee must obtain a detailed description of the child.

2. The employee transmits a Code Adam alert on the nearest in-house telephone or public address system, providing the child's description.

3. Designated employees monitor front entrances while other employees begin looking for the child.

4. If the child is not found within ten minutes, law enforcement is called.

5. If the child is found, and appears to have been lost and unharmed, the child is reunited with his or her family member.

6. If the child is found accompanied by someone other than a parent or legal guardian, reasonable efforts to delay their departure are used without putting the child, staff, or visitors at risk. Law enforcement is again notified and given details about the person accompanying the child.

7. The Code Adam alert is canceled after the child is found or law enforcement arrives.

CODE ADAM PARTICIPANTS

Since its inception, Code Adam has successfully stopped a number of child abductions while they were in progress. The Code Adam program was first implemented in 1994, in approximately 2,500 Wal-Mart Stores and Sam's Clubs. Since that time, through a partnership with the National Center for Missing and Exploited Children (NCMEC), the program has been shared with other companies.

Currently, there are more than 550 Code Adam "partners," and the program has been implemented in 52,000 locations across the country including federal government buildings, as discussed below. All stores, businesses, movie theatres, public buildings, libraries and other establishments are encouraged to adopt the Code Adam program. There is no cost to participate in this program. Businesses can enroll in the program by contacting the NCMEC, as follows:

> National Center for Missing & Exploited Children
> Charles B. Wang International Children's Building
> 699 Prince Street
> Alexandria, Virginia 22314-3175
> Telephone: 703-274-3900
> Fax: 703-274-2200
> Hotline: 1-800-THE-LOST (1-800-843-5678)
> Website: http://www.missingkids.com

The NCMEC will mail the business a free Code Adam kit, consisting of:

1. A training video for the employees;

2. A poster explaining the Adam Code program procedure; and

3. Two Code Adam decals to display at the entrance of the establishment.

A directory of Code Adam participants is set forth at Appendix 7.

THE CODE ADAM ACT OF 2003

To help protect children in federal facilities, the U.S. General Services Administration (GSA), in conjunction with the Federal Protective Service, has adopted the "Code Adam" Program. On April 23, 2003, "The Code Adam Act of 2003" became law.

The Code Adam Act requires the designated authority for a public building to establish procedures for a child missing in a federal facility. The General Services Administration's Public Buildings Service (PBS) administers the federal Code Adam alert program nationwide in both owned and leased buildings, and follows procedures established by the Department of Homeland Security's Federal Protective Service. According to the GSA, following are the steps followed in a federal facility when an alert is announced that a child is missing.

Step 1: Obtain a detailed description of the child, including:

- Name;
- Age;
- Gender;
- Race;
- Weight;
- Height;
- Hair color;
- Eye color; and
- A description of what the child is wearing, specifically the color and type of clothing, including shoe color and style.

Step 2: Report the information about the missing child to the Federal Protective Service or security guards on duty. If there is no security guard on duty, contact the on-site facility manager or delegated official. They will activate the "Code Adam" alert to all building tenants. Also, place a courtesy call to the local police (911) to report the missing child.

Step 3: Security officials will conduct a search of the building. Tenants might be asked to assist with the search. Please cooperate with security.

Step 4: If the child is found with someone other than a parent or guardian, use reasonable efforts to delay the departure of the person accompanying the child, but do not put yourself or others at risk. If possible, notify security officials and describe the identity of the person accompanying the child.

Step 5: When the child is found, bring the child to the security officials or the on-site facility manager. They will reunite the child with their parent or guardian. Security personnel will cancel the "Code Adam" alert. If the child is not found, the security officials or the on-site facility manager will contact the local police again and report any additional information.

CHAPTER 5:
PARENTAL ABDUCTION

IN GENERAL

In most states, it is against the law to keep a child from his or her parent or legal guardian with the intent of depriving that person of custody, even if the person who takes the child also has custodial rights. This may occur, for example, if the custodial parent absconds with the child with the intent of depriving the non-custodial parent from exercising his or her visitation rights, or if the non-custodial parent fails to return the child to the custodial parent following visitation.

In many states, if the child is taken out-of-state, it is a felony. A good faith defense may apply, however, if the parent absconds with the child in order to prevent imminent bodily harm to the child, e.g., physical abuse or sexual molestation. Once one parent takes the child out-of-state, the other parent may be confronted with having to deal with child custody issues across state lines. These issues usually arise when the custodial parent relocates out-of-state in defiance of a court order. As the missing children hotlines and milk carton advertisements demonstrate, a significant number of parents choose to flee with their children rather than allow the courts to determine custody.

A parent often removes a child and drops out of sight completely. Of course, this causes the abandoned parent immense pain and suffering, as well as the financial burden of trying to locate the child and/or litigate custody issues in another state.

FORUM SHOPPING

It is often the absconding parent's intention to relocate in a jurisdiction which he or she feels will render a more favorable determination than would have been made in the child's home state. Of course, this also creates an extreme financial hardship and disadvantage for the other parent who must litigate custody in a distant jurisdiction.

Full faith and credit is a legal principle that requires the court of one state to recognize and enforce valid orders and judgments made by the court of another state. Unfortunately, states often refused to afford full faith and credit to a custody order made by the courts of another state, and would instead make their own custody award. This led to conflicting custody orders, and children would be kidnapped and shuffled back and forth between the two states by the parent wishing to enforce the custody order that was favorable to them in their own state.

As discussed below, two important pieces of legislation—the Uniform Child Custody Jurisdiction Act (UCCJA) and the Parental Kidnapping Prevention Act (PKPA)—were enacted to combat this serious problem of jurisdictional conflict and parental forum shopping in custody decisions. In fact, the UCCJA now requires states to give full faith and credit to the custody orders of other states. Many states have also enacted the Uniform Child-Custody Jurisdiction and Enforcement Act (UCCJEA) to replace the UCCJA, as further discussed below.

The Uniform Child Custody Jurisdiction Act

The Uniform Child Custody Jurisdiction Act of 1968 (UCCJA) has been adopted by all of the states and the District of Columbia. The UCCJA's goal is to eliminate the motives for forum shopping among the states, and to encourage cooperation between state courts. The UCCJA favors awarding jurisdiction to the child's home state, thus deterring parental forum shopping and child snatching. Further, the UCCJA prohibits a state from exercising jurisdiction in a custody action if another state's court has already been involved in the case.

The Uniform Child Custody Jurisdiction Act is set forth at Appendix 8.

The Parental Kidnapping Prevention Act

The Parental Kidnapping Prevention Act of 1980 (PKPA) requires the appropriate authorities of every state to enforce custody and visitation orders made by courts having proper jurisdiction. The PKPA also authorizes the Federal Parental Locator Service to locate children who have been abducted by a parent. Thus, when a parent removes a child from a jurisdiction against court order or contrary to a custody agreement, the lawful custodial parent can obtain federal assistance in locating the child.

In many jurisdictions, the parent who wrongfully takes the child is subject to criminal sanctions for absconding with the child and interfering with custody. Under the PKPA, the Fugitive Felon Act applies to state felony cases involving parental kidnapping and interstate or international flight to avoid prosecution. In such a case, a request for a federal Unlawful Flight to Avoid Prosecution (UFAP) warrant may be filed with the local U.S. Attorney's Office by the state prosecutor.

Relevant provisions of The Parental Kidnapping Act are set forth at Appendix 9.

The Uniform Child-Custody Jurisdiction and Enforcement Act (UCCJEA)

The Uniform Child-Custody Jurisdiction and Enforcement Act (UCCJEA) is a uniform State law that was approved in 1997 by the National Conference of Commissioners on Uniform State Laws (NCCUSL) to replace its 1968 Uniform Child Custody Jurisdiction Act (UCCJA), discussed above. The NCCUSL drafts and proposes laws in areas where it believes uniformity is important, but the laws become effective only upon adoption by state legislatures. As of July 2005, the Act has been enacted by 40 states and the District of Columbia.

A list of jurisdictions that have enacted the Uniform Child-Custody Jurisdiction and Enforcement Act (UCCJEA) is set forth at Appendix 10.

The UCCJEA is designed to deter interstate parental kidnapping and to promote uniform jurisdiction and enforcement provisions in interstate child-custody and visitation cases. The UCCJEA is not a substantive custody statute. It does not dictate standards for making or modifying child custody and visitation decisions; instead, it determines which States' courts have and should exercise jurisdiction to do so.

The UCCJEA is intended to be a complete replacement for the UCCJA in those states that adopt the Act. Articles 1 and 2 of the UCCJEA contain jurisdictional rules that essentially bring the UCCJA into conformity with the PKPA. Modeling the UCCJEA's jurisdictional standards on the PKPA's standards is intended to produce custody determinations that are entitled under Federal law to full faith and credit in sister States. Under articles 1 and 2, the UCCJEA, among other things:

1. Applies to a range of proceedings in which custody or visitation is at issue.

2. Grants priority to home state jurisdiction;

3. Preserves exclusive, continuing jurisdiction in the decree state if that state determines that it has a basis for exercising jurisdiction. Such jurisdiction continues until the child, his or her parents, and any person acting as the child's parent move away from the decree State.

4. Authorizes courts to exercise emergency jurisdiction in cases involving family abuse and limits the relief available in emergency cases to temporary custody orders.

5. Revamps the rules governing inconvenient forum analysis, requiring courts to consider specified factors.

6. Directs courts to decline jurisdiction created by unjustifiable conduct.

The UCCJEA also establishes uniform procedures for interstate enforcement of child custody and visitation determinations. In particular, Article 3 of the UCCJEA:

1. Authorizes temporary enforcement of visitation determinations.

2. Creates an interstate registration process for out-of-State custody determinations.

3. Establishes a procedure for speedy interstate enforcement of custody and visitation determinations.

4. Authorizes issuance of warrants directing law enforcement to pick up children at risk of being removed from the State.

5. Authorizes public officials to assist in the civil enforcement of custody determinations and in Hague Convention cases.

The UCCJEA applies to a variety of proceedings. Specifically, courts in UCCJEA states must comply with the statute when custody and visitation issues arise in proceedings for divorce, separation, neglect, abuse, dependency, guardianship, paternity, termination of parental rights, and protection from domestic violence.

INTERNATIONAL PARENTAL CHILD ABDUCTION

In General

International parental child abduction has become a serious problem in the last several decades. This is due in large part to the relative ease of international travel, and the increase in cross-cultural marriages. The outcome of a custody dispute that crosses international boundaries depends largely on the country to which the parent relocates. The parent left behind must deal with the complexities of foreign law, and the large expense of having to litigate a custody case in a foreign country, where he or she may be confronted with cultural bias favoring the absconding parent with close ties to the country.

Warning Signs

According to the American Bar Association, the chances of an international abduction may increase in the following situations:

1. When the parent has previously abducted the child or threatened to do so;

2. When the parent has no strong ties to the child's home state;

3. When the parent has friends or family living abroad;

4. When the parent has a strong support network;

5. When the parent has no job, can earn a living almost anywhere, or is financially independent;

6. When the parent has recently quit a job, sold a home or terminated a lease, closed a bank account or liquidated other assets;

7. When the parent has a history of marital instability or a lack of parental cooperation;

8. When the parent has a prior criminal record;

9. When the parent feels his or her relationship with the child is threatened; and

10. When the parent has expressed the desire that the child be raised within a certain culture or religion.

Precautions

If you are in a cross-cultural marriage, and fear that your child is vulnerable to abduction, there are a number of precautions you should take, as discussed below.

Dual Citizenship of Child

You should be aware that a child is particularly vulnerable if there is trouble in the marriage, or an impending divorce, and the other parent has close ties with a foreign country. In addition to being a citizen of the United States, they may also have the citizenship of the other parent, if the foreign parent has become a naturalized citizen of the United States. Foreign governments may therefore provide both the parent and child citizens with a passport, visa, and exit or entry permits.

Nevertheless, children under 14 must have both parents' permission to obtain a passport. In addition federal law now requires that each child younger than 14 must appear in person with the parents, and parents must show acceptable identification and proof of parental relationship to the child.

The U.S. Department of State can confirm whether or not a U.S. passport has been issued to your child. If not, you may have your child's information entered into the U.S. Department of State Passport Alert system. Include your child's name, date and place of birth, a copy of any custody order, travel restrictions, and the address and telephone number(s) where you can be reached. If a passport application is subsequently received anywhere in the United States, or in a U.S. Embassy or consulate in a foreign country, the Department of State will notify you. The Department of State may refuse to issue a passport to your child if you have a court order granting you sole custody or requires your written permission to permit the child to travel.

To determine if your child has dual citizenship, contact the embassy or consulate of the foreign parent's country. You should also provide them with a copy of the court order granting you physical custody or restricting your child from being taken out of the United States.

Obtain a Detailed Custody Order

If your spouse has citizenship in a foreign country, it is best to avoid entering into a joint custody order. If the child is abducted to the parent's country, the consulate or embassy may interpret a joint custody order as giving the foreign parent the right to keep the child in the foreign country.

If the court orders joint custody despite your objection, make sure you are listed as the child's primary physical custodian, and that the custody order include your name and address as the place where the child lives most of the time. In addition, specify visitation times and locations. If you fear that abduction is imminent, and the court will not suspend visitation rights, request supervised visitation.

U.S. Department of State Recommendations

In order to prepare for the possibility of an abduction, the United States Department of State has recommended the following precautions:

1. Realize that voluntary travel to the foreign country may result in your child being prevented from returning to the United States. In fact, some foreign countries not only prohibit travel by a child, but also a woman, without the husband's permission. Thus, it is crucial that you inquire about all of the applicable laws and cultural traditions before traveling to a foreign country.

2. Compile information about the other parent to be used in case of an abduction. Keep names and addresses of friends and relatives in the United States and in the foreign country. Maintain a record of the other parent's personal data, such as passport number, social security number, immigration status, visa work permit numbers, and driver's license number, etc.

3. Keep an up-to-date written and detailed description of your child and take color photographs every six months. This information will be very helpful in locating the child if the need should arise. Include your child's hair color, eye color, height, weight, and date of birth.

Also include any unique information that may identify your child, such as the use of eyeglasses or contact lenses, braces, pierced ears, tattoos, and any other special identifying physical attributes.

4. Teach your child what to do in case he or she is removed from the country. For example, teach your child how to use a telephone to call for help.

5. If you are separated or divorced, it is best to obtain a custody decree that incorporates a provision prohibiting your child from traveling out of the United States without your permission. Provide certified copies of the decree to anybody who may be responsible for your child, such as the school, daycare center, camp, and babysitter, etc. Alert them to the possibility that an abduction may take place and instruct them to contact you if there are any unscheduled attempts to retrieve your child.

In addition to the above recommendations, you should also have your child's fingerprints taken by your local law enforcement agency. You should keep the fingerprint card in a safe place as the law enforcement authorities will not keep a copy of your child's fingerprints in their files.

The Hague Convention on the Civil Aspects of International Child Abduction

In General

The Hague Convention on the Civil Aspects of International Child Abduction (The "Hague Convention", adopted by the Hague Conference in 1980, has attempted to combat the problem of international parental child abduction. The Hague Convention's objective is to resolve problems related to international parental child abduction among its member nations by making sure such children are immediately returned to their country of origin. The member nations are referred to in the Convention as "contracting states."

The Hague Convention is set forth at Appendix 11.

Parties to the Hague Convention

In 1988, the United States became a party to the Hague Convention, and implemented legislation providing for the commencement of international child custody litigation under federal law. Its provisions largely mirror the UCCJA and provide procedures for filing international petitions seeking the return of a child, visitation rights, and *habeas corpus* proceedings. As of 2005, 58 countries had become parties to the Hague Convention.

A list of parties to the Hague Convention and their date of entry is set forth at Appendix 12.

Central Authorities

As set forth in Article 6 of the Hague Convention, each contracting state must designate a Central Authority to handle complaints of child abduction, and to cooperate with the Central Authorities of other contracting states to carry out the objectives of the Convention, *i.e.*, secure the prompt return of abducted children. The duties of the Central Authorities in carrying out this objective include:

1. Discovering the whereabouts of the abducted child;

2. Taking such measures necessary to prevent further harm to the child;

3. Securing the voluntary return of the child and amicably resolving the issues;

4. Exchanging information concerning the child;

5. Providing general information concerning its own law as it pertains to the Convention;

6. Initiating judicial or administrative proceedings necessary to secure the return of the child;

7. Providing legal aid and advice to the parties;

8. Providing administrative arrangements necessary to secure the return of the child; and

9. Keeping each other informed and eliminating obstacles that would hinder carrying out the objective of the Convention.

A list of Central Authorities and their websites is set forth at Appendix 13.

Office of Children's Issues (CI)

If you suspect that your child has been abducted to a country that is a party to the Hague Convention, you should contact the Office of Children's Issues (CI), an office of the Overseas Citizens Services (OCS) in the U.S. Department of State. CI works closely with parents, attorneys, other government agencies, and private organizations in the U.S. to prevent international abductions. CI has been designated by Congress as the Central Authority to administer the Hague Convention in the United States.

The Office of Children's Issues can be reached at the following:

U.S. Department of State
Overseas Citizens Services
Office of Children's Issues

2201 C Street NW
Washington, DC 20520
Tel: 1-888-407-4747
Tel: 202-501-4444 (from overseas)

Abduction to Non-Hague Convention Member Countries

If the foreign country to which your child is abducted is not a party to the Hague Convention, you can seek legal remedies against the absconding parent in the federal civil and criminal court systems. Once you suspect that an abduction has occurred, there are a number of steps you can take to locate your child and press charges against the abducting parent:

1. If you have not already done so, seek a custody decree that prohibits your child from traveling without your permission. Without a custody decree granting you sole custody of the child, you will not have legal standing to bring an action.

2. Immediately file a missing person report with the local police department and the National Center for Missing and Exploited Children, and request that the Federal Parent Locator Service attempt a search for the absconding parent.

3. Keep a daily journal detailing the events surrounding your child's abduction to help you remember the events exactly as they occurred. Record contact names and telephone numbers.

4. Request the Department of State, Overseas Citizens Services, Office of Children's Issues (CI) to initiate a welfare and whereabouts search for your child overseas.

5. Inform the embassy and consulates of the country to which you suspect your child has been taken of your custody decree. Instruct them not to issue a foreign passport or visa to your child.

6. Check the U.S. Passport Agency to see whether a passport has been issued in your child's name.

7. If your child is school age, contact his or her school officials and ask to be informed if anyone requests a transfer of your child's records.

8. Contact your child's medical providers and have them flag your child's medical records in case anyone requests copies.

9. Try and track down the absconding parent through personal contacts and records, e.g., friends and relatives, and credit card and telephone bills.

10. Once your child has been located, retain an attorney in the foreign jurisdiction.

11. Seek to have an arrest warrant under state and/or federal statutes issued for the arrest of the absconding parent.

12. Once the arrest warrant has been issued, have the absconding parent's name registered with the National Crime Information Center (NCIS) and, if a U.S. citizen, seek to have his or her passport revoked. Consider whether extradition would be possible.

CHAPTER 6:
INTERNET SAFETY

IN GENERAL

The Internet has changed the way children learn, communicate, social-ize and play. Unfortunately, it has also opened up countless outlets for predatory behavior. Adults join chat rooms, online gaming areas, and other websites designed for minors, and pose as peers in order to gain the confidence of children and trick them into divulging personal iden-tifying information.

Online predators spend a considerable amount of time trying to seduce children by gradually introducing sexual topics in chat rooms, at-tempting to prey upon the child's natural curiosity about sexuality. Unsuspecting minors are lured to malls and other meeting places where they are quickly victimized by these child predators. Thus, par-ents must take every precaution available to protect their children while they are using this valuable resource.

RECOGNIZE THE WARNING SIGNS

Many children visit Internet sites to socialize with their peers and share common interests. Unfortunately, child predators also visit the same sites in order to target their victims. Therefore, it is important to educate yourself about Internet usage and monitor the websites and chat rooms your child visits. To properly monitor your child's online activities, your computer should be located in an area of your home where you can see what your child is doing when they are online.

If your child is spending an excessive amount of time online, particu-larly at night, this may indicate that your child is at risk. Chat rooms are the most dangerous areas on the Internet. Many children enter chat rooms to meet and converse with their peers. Children who spend a lot of time in chat rooms are more likely to be contacted by child pred-ators, who often work during the day and spend their evening hours searching the Internet for potential victims. According to recent statistics, 65% of online incidents occur in chat rooms, and 24% occur while the child is using Instant Messaging.

The problem is that child predators often pose as children when they are in the chat rooms. The child may think they are conversing with another child when an adult predator is really contacting them. Chat rooms fulfill the predator's need to communicate with children, and enable the pedophile to identify vulnerable children and recruit them into sexually illicit relationships. In addition to the chat rooms, child predators may attempt to contact your child through e-mail and instant messaging (IM).

In order to monitor your child's online activities, it is advisable to locate the computer in an area where it can be monitored easily, such as in the family room. You can also monitor your child's online activity by checking their bookmarks, cache, or history. In addition, you should learn the online acronyms children use when communicating on the Internet so you can understand the content of the messages being exchanged.

A list of online acronyms is set forth at Appendix 14.

If your child begins to withdraw from family activities, choosing instead to spend time in online chat rooms, it may indicate that the predator is trying to alienate the child from the family. Child predators often try to side with the child in disputes with his or her parents, in an effort to trick the child into trusting the predator, and cause a rift between the child and his or her family.

If you find pornography on your child's computer, it is possible that your child has been contacted by a child predator. Predators often e-mail pornographic images to potential victims to try and lure them into sexually explicit conversations, and to make them feel comfortable with sexual images and concepts.

If your child turns off the computer monitor as soon as you walk in the room, it is likely that there is something on the screen that he or she does not want you to see. It is advisable to routinely search your child's computer files and CDs/disks for illicit material.

If your child starts making and/or receiving telephone calls to and/or from unrecognizable telephone numbers, it is possible that a child predator has obtained your child's phone number or given your child his or her telephone number. The child predator's next move after making online contact with the child is making telephone contact, e.g., to engage in phone sex or try to set up a face-to-face meeting.

It is advisable to monitor your Caller ID numbers to determine whether there have been any calls from an unknown number. You can also purchase a device that will list the telephone numbers of all calls placed from your telephone. In addition, you should consider obtaining a "call block" or "call reject" feature from your telephone company, thereby preventing the predator from obtaining your telephone number, and rejecting their anonymous calls.

If your child nevertheless receives a phone call from an adult, you must find out who the person is, how your child knows the individual, and the content of the telephone conversation. If your child starts to receive gifts or letters from a stranger, again, you must find out all of the details about the sender. Child predators often try to seduce children with presents. If you discover that a stranger is trying to set up a meeting with your child, contact your local law enforcement agency immediately. Keep the items in case they are needed as evidence in any subsequent criminal case against the perpetrator.

If you find out that your child has been sexually solicited by an adult, or has received sexually explicit e-mails or images, you should immediately contact your local law enforcement agency, the FBI, and the National Center for Missing and Exploited Children. Preserve the computer files so that the appropriate authorities can inspect the material. If your child did engage in any sexual activity with the predator, realize that your child is a victim, even if he or she was a willing participant, and focus the blame on the child predator.

REDUCE THE RISKS

Set Guidelines

In order to reduce the risk of your child becoming victimized by a child predator, you and your child should thoroughly discuss the dangers existing on the Internet, and set guidelines they must adhere to when using the Internet, as follows:

1. Do not arrange a meeting with someone you meet online;

2. Do not post pictures of yourself onto the Internet or send pictures via e-mail to anyone you do not know;

3. Do not open unsolicited e-mails, particularly if the e-mail contains images;

4. Do not give out your personal identifying information, such as your name, address, telephone number, or school name as child predators have been able to identify, locate and track children using the information they acquired online; and

5. Do not respond to angry, intimidating, obscene, or sexually explicit e-mails.

Also, tell your child to let you know if they receive any inappropriate contact while they are online. If the contact is particularly disturbing, alert the website and consider reporting the incident to local law enforcement.

Some parents choose to ban their children from using the Internet, however, this is not necessary. If you educate your child about the dangers, monitor their usage, and implement parental controls and other available safeguards, your child will certainly benefit from the wealth of information available online.

Blocking, Filtering and Parental Controls

There are services available that rate websites for content, filter programming, and enable you to block sites you consider inappropriate for your child to visit. These programs all work differently. For example, some programs block websites considered inappropriate for children, and some prevent users from entering personal identifying information, such as their name and address. Parental controls allow you to keep your children out of chat rooms, and/or restrict your child's ability to send or read E-mail. Try to configure your blocking, filtering and parental controls features so that they do not block websites that you want your child to be able to access, such as educational websites, etc. Nevertheless, be aware that blocking and filtering programs are not 100% foolproof.

Review Website Privacy Policies

Websites often ask for personal information so that they can gather marketing information concerning the users who visit their website. The information gathered may also be shared with others for marketing and other purposes. Privacy policies vary among websites; therefore, parents are advised to read them carefully.

It is important to determine whether the website your child visits has a privacy policy. If so, the privacy policy should detail the following:

1. The type of information collected;

2. How the information is used;

3. Whether the information is shared with third parties; and

4. What control the user has over their personal information.

Privacy policies should also advise the user how they can find out what information has been collected by the website so that erroneous information can be corrected or deleted. The privacy policy should also explain how the company restricts their employees' access to the user's personal information.

Users may also have the choice to "opt out" of having their information used in various ways. If there is such an "opt out" policy, the user must generally affirmatively state that they do not want their information used. Otherwise, the information will be disseminated, meaning that it will be used unless you say "no." If there is an "opt in" policy, this means that the user's personal information cannot be used unless they affirmatively state that they want their information used.

Many websites also ask for the user's permission to contact them in the future by e-mail with notices, updates, offers and other information. The user should have the option of declining permission for future contact.

One way of knowing whether or not a website is using a security system is to watch the address bar on the screen. At the point where the user enters their personal information, the prefix on the address should change to "shttp" or "https." Scroll left to determine whether the prefix changed. If you are unsure, contact the website directly to find out about their online security system and privacy policy. If the website states that your personal identifying does not need to be encrypted, do not permit your child to patronize the website.

Cookies

The term "cookies" refers to bits of electronic information that identify the computer used by a specific user to a particular website. Cookies are placed on a user's computer when he or she visits various websites. Cookies are used by the website to tailor information to the particular user, such as marketing information, preferences, etc. Cookies are also used so that users can easily access the website without having to enter their password each time they visit the site.

The presence of cookies on a website can be detected using special software or particular browser settings. To check for cookie files on your computer, search the hard drive for a file labeled "cookies.txt." You can then delete the cookie files if you do not want to keep them on your computer's hard drive.

THE INNOCENT IMAGES NATIONAL INITIATIVE

In May 1993, FBI agents were investigating the disappearance of a child. During the course of the investigation, the agents discovered two suspects who had been engaged in the sexual exploitation of children over a 25-year period. The suspects routinely used computers to send sexually explicit images to the children, and lure the children into engaging in illicit sexual activity.

It was further discovered that computer telecommunication was rapidly becoming one of the most prevalent techniques by which child predators engaged in these illicit activities. In order to address this serious problem, the Innocent Images National Initiative (IINI) was instituted as a component of the FBI's Cyber Crimes Program.

IINI undercover operations are conducted in several FBI field offices by task forces that combine the resources of the FBI with other federal, state and local law enforcement agencies. International investigations are coordinated through the FBI's Legal Attaché program, which coordinates investigations with the appropriate foreign law enforcement.

IINI investigations are also coordinated with Internet Crimes Against Children (ICAC) Task Forces, which are funded by the Department of Justice. In addition, IINI training is provided to all law enforcement agencies involved in IINI investigations, including federal, state, local, and foreign law enforcement agencies.

Mission

The IINI's mission is to: (i) reduce the vulnerability of children to acts of sexual exploitation and abuse which are facilitated through the use of computers; (ii) identify and rescue witting and unwitting child victims; (iii) investigate and prosecute sexual predators who use the Internet and other online services to sexually exploit children for personal or financial gain; and (iv) strengthen the capabilities of federal, state, local, and international law enforcement through training programs and investigative assistance.

The IINI focuses its investigative and prosecutorial efforts on:

1. Online Organizations, enterprises, and communities that exploit children for profit or personal gain;

2. Individuals who travel, or indicate a willingness to travel, for the purpose of engaging in sexual activity with a minor;

3. Producers of child pornography;

4. Major distributors of child pornography; and

5. Possessors of child pornography.

The IINI has also established a law enforcement presence on the Internet to act as a deterrent to those who seek to sexually exploit children. The IINI investigates all areas of the Internet and online services including:

1. Internet websites that post child pornography;

2. Internet News Groups;

3. Internet Relay Chat (IRC);

4. Bulletin Board Systems (BBSs); and

5. Peer-to-Peer (P2P) file-sharing programs

FBI agents and task force officers go online undercover into these locations utilizing fictitious screen names and engaging in real-time chat or E-mail conversations with suspected predators to obtain evidence of criminal activity. Investigation of specific online locations can be initiated through:

1. A citizen complaint;

2. A complaint by an online service provider;

3. A referral from a law enforcement agency; and

4. The suspicion that the name of the online location suggests illicit activity.

IINI Child Sex Crimes Investigation

The most common crimes investigated under the IINI are in violation of Title 18 United States Code (USC):

1. Importation or Transportation of Obscene Matters (18 U.S.C. §1462);

2. Transportation of Obscene Matters for Sale or Distribution (18 U.S.C. §1465);

3. Engaging in the Business of Selling or Transferring Obscene Matter (18 U.S.C. §1466);

4. Transfer of Obscene Material to Minors (18 U.S.C. §1470);

5. Aggravated Sexual Abuse (18 U.S.C. §2241(a)(b)(c));

6. Sexual Exploitation of Children (18 U.S.C. §2251(a)(b)(c));

7. Selling or Buying of Children (18 U.S.C. §2251A(a)(b));

8. Certain Activities Relating to Material Involving the Sexual Exploitation of Minors (18 U.S.C. §2252);

9. Certain Activities Relating to Material Constituting or Containing Child Pornography (18 U.S.C. §2252A)—Child Pornography has been defined as a visual depiction of a minor—*i.e.*, a child younger than 18—engaged in sexually explicit conduct;

10. Production of Sexually Explicit Depictions of a Minor for Importation into the U.S. (18 U.S.C. §2260(a)(b));

11. Coercion and Enticement (18 U.S.C. §2422);

12. Transportation of Minors with Intent to Engage in Criminal Sexual Activity (18 U.S.C. §2423(a));

13. Interstate or Foreign Travel with Intent to Engage in a Sexual Act with a Juvenile (18 U.S.C. §2423(b)); and

14. Use of Interstate Facilities to Transmit Information about a Minor (18 U.S.C. §2425);

15. Misleading Domain Name (18 U.S.C. 2252B).

IINI Endangered Child Alert Program

On February 21, 2004, the FBI began its Endangered Child Alert Program (ECAP), an aggressive approach to identify unknown individuals involved in the sexual abuse of children and production of child pornography. The ECAP uses national and international media exposure of unknown adults featured in child pornography and displays their face on the "Seeking Information" section of the FBI's website (www.fbi.gov/mostwant/seekinfo/seekcac.htm/). The FBI encourages the public to view the photos and identify the perpetrators. If the perpetrator is not identified through the FBI website, they are broadcast on the television show "America's Most Wanted: America Fights Back."

IINI Operation Peer Pressure

In November 2003, the FBI initiated Phase I of "Operation Peer Pressure," a nationwide initiative to target users of Peer-to-Peer (P2P) networks to collect and distribute child pornography. Peer-to-Peer networks are free file-sharing programs that allow users to find and exchange files from other users with the same Internet software.

Once a user installs a Peer-to-Peer software application, they can directly access and search for files in designated folders on other user's computers. During this phase, the FBI conducted online sessions in which undercover FBI Agents downloaded child pornography from pedophile's computers. As of January 4, 2006, the FBI has executed over 300 searches, 69 subjects were indicted, and over 40 convictions have been achieved.

It is important for parents to be educated about the risks associated with peer-to-peer networking. Parents should be aware that access to these networks is free, and exposure to child pornography is not uncommon. The sense of anonymity of the network encourages pedophiles to share their pornographic material to a wide audience. In addition, pedophiles often use popular search terms to expose innocent children to graphic pornographic images. For example, a child may search a Peer-to-Peer network for their favorite singer, and retrieve child pornography instead.

Additional information on the FBI Innocent Images National Initiative may be obtained from the FBI at the following address:

Federal Bureau of Investigation
Cyber Division
Innocent Images National Initiative
11700 Beltsville Drive
Calverton, MD 20705

CYBERTIPLINE

The National Center for Missing and Exploited Children (NCMEC) operates a CyberTipline that allows parents and children to report child pornography and other incidents of sexual exploitation of children by submitting an online form (www.cybertipline.com). The NCMEC also maintains a 24-hour hotline of 1-800-THE-LOST and a website (www.missingkids.com).

Complaints received by the NCMEC that indicate a violation of federal law are referred to the FBI for appropriate action. FBI analysts are assigned full-time at the NCMEC to assist with these complaints. The analysts review and analyze information received by the CyberTipline in order to identify individuals suspected of any of the following: (i) possession, manufacture and/or distribution of child pornography; (ii) online enticement of children for sexual acts; (iii) child sexual tourism; and (iv) other sexual exploitation of children.

Once a potential suspect has been identified, an investigative packet is compiled consisting of the CyberTipline reports, subpoena results, public records search results, the illegal images associated with the suspect, and the packet is sent to the appropriate FBI field office for investigation. Reports are also sent to the appropriate Internet Service Providers.

Further information may be obtained by contacting the NCMEC as follows:

The National Center for Missing & Exploited Children (NCMEC)
Charles B. Wang International Children's Building
699 Prince Street
Alexandria, VA 22314
Website: www.cybertipline.com
24-Hour Hotline: 1-800-THE-LOST (1-800-843-5678)

THE CHILDREN'S ONLINE PRIVACY PROTECTION ACT (COPPA)

The Children's Online Privacy Protection Act (COPPA) and the FTC's implementing Rule took effect April 21, 2000. The primary goal of the Act and the Rule is to place parents in control over what information is collected from their children online.

The COPPA Rule applies to individually identifiable information about a child such as name, home address, e-mail address, telephone number or any other information that would allow someone to identify or contact the child. The Act also covers other types of information, such as hobbies, interests and information collected through "cookies" or other types of tracking mechanisms when they are tied to individually identifiable information.

The COPPA Rule applies to operators of commercial websites and online services directed to children under 13 that collect personal information from children, and operators of general audience sites with actual knowledge that they are collecting information from children under 13.

The COPPA Rule sets out a number of factors in determining whether a website is targeted to children, including:

1. The website's subject matter;

2. The website's language;

3. The website's use of animated characters; and

4. Whether advertising appearing on the website is directed to children.

The Commission will also consider empirical evidence regarding the ages of the website's visitors. These standards are very similar to those previously established for TV, radio, and print advertising.

The COPPA Rule requires the website operator to post a link to a notice of its information practices on the home page of its website or online service and at each area where it collects personal information from children. An operator of a general audience site with a separate children's area must post a link to its notice on the home page of the children's area.

The link to the privacy notice must be clear and prominent. The notice must be clearly written and understandable. It should not include any unrelated or confusing materials. It must state the following information:

1. The name and contact information, including address, telephone number and e-mail address, of all operators collecting or maintain-

ing children's personal information through the website or online service. If more than one operator is collecting information, the website may select and provide contact information for only one operator who will respond to all inquiries from parents about the website's privacy policies. However, the names of all operators must be listed in the notice.

2. The kinds of personal information collected from children and how the information is collected—e.g., directly from the child, or passively through "cookies."

3. How the operator uses the personal information.

4. Whether the operator discloses information collected from children to third parties. If so, the operator also must disclose: (i) the kinds of businesses in which the third parties are engaged; (ii) the general purposes for which the information is used; and (iii) whether the third parties have agreed to maintain the confidentiality and security of the information.

5. That the parent has the option to agree to the collection and use of the child's information without consenting to the disclosure of the information to third parties.

6. That the operator may not require a child to disclose more information than is reasonably necessary to participate in an activity as a condition of participation.

7. That the parent can review the child's personal information, ask to have it deleted and refuse to allow any further collection or use of the child's information. The notice also must state the procedures for the parent to follow to do so.

The notice to parents must contain the same information included on the notice on the website. In addition, an operator must notify a parent that it wishes to collect personal information from the child; that the parent's consent is required for the collection, use and disclosure of the information; and how the parent can provide consent. The notice to parents must be written clearly and understandably, and must not contain any unrelated or confusing information. An operator may use any one of a number of methods to notify a parent, including sending an e-mail message to the parent or a notice by regular mail.

Before collecting, using or disclosing personal information from a child, an operator must obtain verifiable parental consent from the child's parent. This means an operator must make reasonable efforts to ensure that the child's parent receives notice of the operator's information practices, and consents to those practices, before any personal information is collected from the child.

Operators may use e-mail to get parental consent for all internal uses of personal information, such as marketing back to a child based on his or her preferences or communicating promotional updates about site content, as long as they take additional steps to increase the likelihood that the parent has, in fact, provided the consent.

An operator must give a parent the option to agree to the collection and use of the child's personal information without agreeing to the disclosure of the information to third parties. However, when a parent agrees to the collection and use of their child's personal information, the operator may release that information to others who use it solely to provide support for the internal operations of the website or service, including technical support and order fulfillment.

The regulations include several exceptions that allow operators to collect a child's e-mail address without getting the parent's consent in advance. These exceptions cover many popular online activities for kids, including contests, online newsletters, homework help and electronic postcards. Prior parental consent is not required when:

1. An operator collects a child's or parent's e-mail address to provide notice and seek consent;

2. An operator collects an e-mail address to respond to a one-time request from a child and then deletes it;

3. An operator collects an e-mail address to respond more than once to a specific request in which case the operator must notify the parent that it is communicating regularly with the child and give the parent the opportunity to stop the communication before sending or delivering a second communication to a child;

4. An operator collects a child's name or online contact information to protect the safety of a child who is participating on the website in which case the operator must notify the parent and give him or her the opportunity to prevent further use of the information;

5. An operator collects a child's name or online contact information to protect the security or liability of the website or to respond to law enforcement, if necessary, and does not use it for any other purpose.

An operator is required to send a new notice and request for consent to parents if there are material changes in the collection, use or disclosure practices to which the parent had previously agreed.

At a parent's request, operators must disclose the general kinds of personal information they collect online from children as well as the specific information collected from children who visit their websites. Operators must use reasonable procedures to ensure they are dealing with the child's parent before they provide access to the child's specific information. They can use a variety of methods to verify the parent's identity, including:

1. Obtaining a signed form from the parent via regular mail or fax;

2. Accepting and verifying a credit card number;

3. Taking calls from parents on a toll-free telephone number staffed by trained personnel;

4. E-mail accompanied by digital signature;

5. E-mail accompanied by a PIN or password obtained through one of the verification methods above.

Operators who follow one of these procedures acting in good faith to a request for parental access are protected from liability under federal and state law for inadvertent disclosures of a child's information to someone who purports to be a parent.

At any time, a parent may revoke his or her consent, refuse to allow an operator to further use or collect their child's personal information, and direct the operator to delete the information. In turn, the operator may terminate any service provided to the child, but only if the information at issue is reasonably necessary for the child's participation in that activity. If other activities on the website do not require the child's e-mail address, the operator must allow the child access to those activities.

The Federal Trade Commission (FTC) monitors the Internet for compliance with the Rule and brings law enforcement actions where appropriate to deter violations. Parents and other concerned individuals can submit complaints to the FTC for investigation. The FTC will also investigate referrals from consumer groups, industry, and approved safe harbor programs, as appropriate.

The FTC may impose civil penalties for violations of the Rule in the same manner as for other Rules under the FTC Act. The level of penalties assessed may turn on a number of factors including egregiousness of the violation. The factors considered may include:

1. the number of children involved;

2. the amount and type of personal information collected;

3. how the information was used;

4. whether the information was shared with third parties; and

5. the size of the company.

The FTC has set up a special web page designed for children, parents, businesses, and educators (http://www.ftc.gov/kidzprivacy/).

In addition to providing compliance materials for businesses and parents, this web page features online safety tips for children and other useful education resources about the Children's Online Privacy Protection Act and related rules and online privacy in general.

The Children's Online Privacy Protection Act (COPPA) is set forth at Appendix 15.

THE CHILDREN'S INTERNET PROTECTION ACT

The Children's Internet Protection Act (CIPA) is a federal law enacted by Congress in December 2000 to address concerns about access to offensive content over the Internet on school and library computers. CIPA imposes certain types of requirements on any school or library that receives funding support for Internet access or internal connections from the "E-rate" program—a program that makes certain technology more affordable for eligible schools and libraries.

Schools and libraries subject to CIPA may not receive the discounts offered by the E-Rate program unless they certify that they have an Internet safety policy and technology protection measures in place. An Internet safety policy must include technology protection measures to block or filter Internet access to pictures that are: (a) obscene; (b) child pornography, or (c) harmful to minors, for computers that are accessed by minors.

In addition, schools subject to CIPA are required to adopt and enforce a policy to monitor online activities of minors; and to adopt and implement a policy addressing the following:

1. access by minors to inappropriate matter on the Internet;

2. the safety and security of minors when using electronic mail, chat rooms, and other forms of direct electronic communications;

3. unauthorized access, including so-called "hacking," and other unlawful activities by minors online;

4. unauthorized disclosure, use, and dissemination of personal information regarding minors; and

5. restricting minors' access to materials harmful to them.

Schools and libraries are required to certify that they have their safety policies and technology in place before receiving E-rate funding. Nevertheless, CIPA does not affect E-rate funding for schools and libraries receiving discounts only for telecommunications, such as telephone service.

An authorized person may disable the blocking or filtering measure during any use by an adult to enable access for *bona fide* research or other lawful purposes. In addition, CIPA does not require the tracking of Internet use by minors or adults.

The Children's Internet Protection Act (CIPA) is set forth at Appendix 16.

CHAPTER 7:
SEXUAL EXPLOITATION OF CHILDREN

IN GENERAL

All children are vulnerable to sexual exploitation. The sexual victimization of children is overwhelming in magnitude yet largely unrecognized and underreported. Statistics show that 1 in 5 girls and 1 in 10 boys are sexually exploited before they reach adulthood, yet less than 35% of those child sexual assaults are reported to authorities. Sexual exploitation can take many forms, including child molestation; child pornography; child prostitution; child sex tourism; online child enticement, etc.

CHILD MOLESTATION

Child molesters are masters of child manipulation. They often "groom" a child with affection, and lure them with gifts. Their "public" face is often that of a decent, law-abiding citizen, a role they play in order to gain the trust of the child as well as his or her parents. It is when they succeed in gaining this trust that they strike. An act of child molestation can include:

1. inappropriate touching or fondling;

2. exposing their private parts to children—*i.e.*, "flashing;"

3. engaging in sexual activity with the child, *e.g.* vaginal, anal or oral sex;

4. showing child pornography to a child; and

5. forcing the child to participate in, or witness, deviant sexual behaviors.

Warning Signs

It is difficult to prevent every harm that may befall your child, however, there are some preventive measures you can take to reduce the risks.

Keep an open line of communication with your child so he or she feels comfortable speaking with you about any topic. Talk to them about safety, and their right to report situations that make them uncomfortable, such as inappropriate touching by an adult.

Watch for any unusual attention being given to your child by an adult, such as gifts or the desire to spend time with your child. Also, carefully check all of the references of any individuals you hire who will be working in close proximity to your children, including babysitters, household help, repair persons, maintenance persons, etc.

There is usually some type of change in a child's behavior if he or she has been sexually molested due to the often devastating physical and emotional trauma the child has sustained. However, many children, either out of fear or embarrassment, do not report the incident to their parents or other authority figures. You should monitor your child's behavior carefully, particularly if there is any chance your child has been molested. Your child should be encouraged to discuss their feelings openly to start the healing process.

Although there may also be benign reasons for similar behaviors, the following are warning signs that may indicate your child has been sexually molested:

1. an extreme change in your child's behavior, *e.g.*, aggression, misbehavior in school, etc.;

2. excessive and atypical episodes of fear, crying, and mood swings that are atypical for your child;

3. sudden sleep disturbances, including nightmares, bed-wetting, and regressive behaviors;

4. an unusual interest in sexual topics and inappropriate sexual behavior, particularly if your child has not previously exhibited any such interests;

5. unexplained injuries, especially in the genital area.

Children who have been victimized by child molesters, and survive the traumatic experience, suffer long-lasting debilitating effects, often on into adulthood. Studies indicate that the physical and mental trauma caused by the abuse often results in severe depression, anger, and psychological disorders, including post-traumatic stress disorder. These children suffer guilt and low self-esteem, nightmares, and flashbacks, and a negative impact on their own sexual growth and normalcy.

If you find that your child has been the victim of child molestation, seek immediate medical attention for your child, and contact law enforcement and other appropriate authorities. In addition, your child will likely need some type of counseling to deal with the traumatic after-effects. Contact a therapist who is thoroughly familiar with child victims of sexual assault.

CHILD PORNOGRAPHY

All states, the District of Columbia, and the federal government have laws that make it illegal to possess, distribute, or manufacture child pornography.

A table of state child pornography statutes is set forth at Appendix 17.

Federal law defines child pornography as any visual depiction, including any photograph, film, video, or computer or computer-generated image or picture, whether made or produced by electronic, mechanical, or other means, of sexually explicit conduct, where:

1. the production of such visual depiction involves the use of a minor engaging in sexually explicit conduct;

2. such visual depiction is a digital image, computer image, or computer-generated image that is, or is indistinguishable from, that of a minor engaging in sexually explicit conduct; or

3. such visual depiction has been created, adapted, or modified to appear that an identifiable minor is engaging in sexually explicit conduct.

A "visual depiction of any kind," includes a drawing, cartoon, sculpture, or painting, photograph, film, video, or computer or computer-generated image or picture, whether made or produced by electronic, mechanical, or other means. "Sexually explicit conduct" includes various forms of sexual activity, such as intercourse, bestiality, masturbation, sadistic or masochistic abuse, and lascivious exhibition of the genitals.

Possession and Distribution of Child Pornography

It is illegal for any person to knowingly possess or attempt to possess child pornography, transport or mail child pornography, or otherwise attempt to disseminate pornographic images of children, including dissemination over the Internet.

Child pornographers target all ages of children, including infants. According to the National Juvenile Online Victimization Study (NCMEC 2005), of those individuals arrested in the United States for the possession of child pornography between 2000 and 2001, 83% had images involving children between ages 6 and 12; 39% had images involving children between ages 3 and 5; and 19% had images of infants and toddlers under 3 years of age.

Dual Offenders

According to the National Center for Missing and Exploited Children (NCMEC), a June 2005 study reported that 40% of arrested child pornography possessors had both sexually victimized children and were in possession of child pornography. These offenders are also known as "dual offenders." Both crimes were discovered in the same investigation. Another 15% were "dual offenders" who tried to victimize children by soliciting undercover investigators who posed as minors online. Overall 36% of "dual offenders" showed or gave child pornography to identified victims or undercover investigators posing as minors online.

Child Pornography on the Internet

Pornographic images of children have been distributed throughout the world via the Internet, encompassing a massive underground industry. The statistics are staggering:

1. According to the National Society for the Prevention of Cruelty to Children, more than 20,000 images of child pornography are posted on the Internet every week.

2. According to researchers who monitored the Internet over a six-week period, 140,000 child pornography images were posted during that time period.

3. According to a National Children's Homes report, the number of Internet child pornography images has increased by 1,500% since 1988.

4. According to a study entitled Internet Sex Crimes Against Minors: The Response of Law Enforcement (NCMEC 2003), 20% of all Internet pornography involves children.

5. The U.S. Customs Service estimates that there are more than 100,000 websites offering child pornography, and revenue estimates for the industry range from about $200 million to more than $1 billion per year.

Child sexual predators use computers to organize large databases of unlawful pornographic images, which they share amongst their fellow predators. Often they include their own illegal acts of child molestation in their collection, which is distributed throughout the Internet, and there is presently no way of retrieving these images, which continue to circulate.

Obviously, the children who are sexually abused for purposes of manufacturing child pornography are the primary individual victims of this despicable crime, suffering long-lasting severe physical and emotional injuries. As these images continue to circulate, they are re-victimized over and over again.

However, an even larger segment of the child population is also at risk. Children who are innocently exploring the Internet for legitimate purposes, e.g., homework, research project, etc., may easily be exposed to pornography, including pornographic sexual images of other children.

If you or your child accidentally encounter child pornography online, you should immediately contact your Internet service provider. Internet service providers are required by law to report any violations to the CyberTipline operated by the National Center for Missing and Exploited Children (NCMECEC) as soon as is reasonably possible.

ONLINE ENTICEMENT BY SEXUAL PREDATORS

As discussed in Chapter 6 of this almanac, the Internet has opened up a whole new way for children to learn and communicate, however, it has also attracted child sexual predators who now have direct contact with this vulnerable population upon whom they prey, and an outlet for their perverse activities.

Online enticement refers to the use of the Internet to entice, invite, or persuade a child to meet for sexual acts or to help arrange such a meeting. According to Highlights of the Youth Internet Safety Survey conducted by the U.S. Department of Justice, one in five children aged 10 to 17 has received an unwanted sexual solicitation online. Law enforcement officials estimate that as many as 50,000 sexual predators are online at any given moment, and the National Criminal Intelligence Service reports that these pedophiles are increasingly adopting counter-intelligence techniques to protect themselves from being traced by law enforcement authorities.

Online sexual predators spend a considerable amount of time trying to seduce children by gradually introducing sexual topics in chat rooms, and often begin e-mailing sexual images directly to a specific child, attempting to prey upon the child's natural curiosity about sexuality. It is the intent of the sexual predator to expose the child victim to multiple images of their peers engaged in sexual activity, in an attempt to lower the child's inhibitions by portraying this behavior as "normal." Unsuspecting minors are then lured to malls and other meeting places where they are quickly victimized by these child predators.

The CyberTipline is a congressionally-mandated reporting mechanism for cases of child sexual exploitation including pornographic images of children, online enticement of children for sex acts, molestation of children outside the family, sex tourism of children, child victims of prostitution, and unsolicited obscene material sent to a child. Reports may be made 24-hours per day, 7 days per week online at www.cybertipline.com or by calling 1-800-843-5678.

Chapter 6 discusses the importance of monitoring your child's online activities, and the various ways you can make the Internet safer for your child.

CHILD PROSTITUTION

Child prostitution involves the sexual exploitation of a child in exchange for some type of compensation. Hundreds of thousands of children, both male and female, have been lured into prostitution. The dangers children face as a result of prostitution are both immediate and long-term. Immediate and obvious dangers are the physical, mental, and emotional injuries these children suffer at the hands of their perpetrators. The long-term effects include long-term psychological problems, serious health concerns, drug and alcohol addiction, and even murder or suicide.

These children come from all walks of life, small towns, suburbs and urban areas, and they come from all income levels. Most are girls, although researchers have indicated an increase in the number of boys involved in child prostitution. Studies have found a link between child prostitution and runaway children. Children who leave home and are lured into prostitution are often victims of prior physical, emotional or sexual abuse, often occurring within their household. Predators use this vulnerability to lure these youths by offering affection, attention and what the child perceives as "love." Once the sexual predator gains their confidence, the child performs acts of prostitution in order to maintain his or her relationship with the predator.

The average age a child enters prostitution is 14, although the child may be victimized as young as 9 years of age. Anyone who engages in sexual activity with a minor is guilty of statutory rape, regardless of whether the child made the advance. Pursuant to the federal law prohibiting sexual abuse of a minor (18 U.S.C. § 2243), it is a crime to engage in sexual acts with any individual who is not yet 12 years of age, or engage in sexual acts with any individual who is older than 12 but not yet 16 years of age with at least a four-year difference in age. All states have similar prohibitions.

A table of state statutory ages for sexual consent is set forth at Appendix 18.

Children who are lured into prostitution are often taken far away from their home in order to avoid detection and keep the child secluded. The "Mann Act" is a federal law that prohibits the transportation, or attempted transportation, of a child under the age of 18 in interstate or foreign commerce, with the intent that the child engage in prostitution or any sexual activity for which any person can be charged with a criminal offense. All states and the District of Columbia have enacted similar laws.

CHILD SEX TOURISM

Child sex tourism is defined as traveling to a foreign country with the intent to engage in sexual activity with a child younger than the age of 18. Although many countries have a reputation for this type of illegal activity, child sex tourism occurs in just about every country in the world.

Despite efforts to stop child sex tourism, sexual predators continue to engage in this activity because it is available, affordable, they can do so anonymously, and the foreign countries where it occurs lack and/or fail to enforce child protection laws. Due to the Internet, child sex predators are able to share their experiences and offer advice to their fellow pedophiles.

It is against the law for any citizen of the United States to engage in child sex tourism and, individuals who do so, are subject to prosecution in the United States, as follows:

Travel With Intent to Engage in Sexual Acts with a Juvenile (18 U.S.C. § 2423B)

A person who travels in interstate commerce, or conspires to do so, or a citizen of the United States or an alien admitted for permanent residence in the United States who travels in foreign commerce, or conspires to do so, for the purpose of engaging in a sexual act with a person [younger than] 18 years of age that would be in violation of chapter 109A if the sexual act occurred in the special maritime and territorial jurisdiction of the United States shall be fined under this title, imprisoned not more than 10 years, or both.

THE CHILDREN'S SAFETY ACT OF 2005 (H.R. 3132)

The Children's Safety Act of 2005 has been passed in the House and is presently pending a vote in the Senate. If the legislation passes, it will be a huge step in protecting children from sexual predators. Major provisions of the proposed Act include the following:

1. The Act will create a comprehensive, national system for sex offender registration.

2. The Act will improve information exchange between states when sex offenders move from state to state.

3. The Act will increase penalties on offenders for failing to comply with the registration law.

4. The Act will require all states to have a website containing information about all sex offenders.

5. The Act will require changes in registry information immediately, electronically transmitted to all states.

6. The Act will require law enforcement notification of schools, child welfare agencies, and youth-service organizations, etc., regarding the presence of a sex offender in the area.

7. The Act will require lifetime registration for offenders with felony convictions.

8. The Act will require an increased penalty for failure to register or verify to a state felony, with a minimum of 1 year in prison and, in some cases, a federal felony, with possible 5–20 years in federal prison.

9. The Act will require offenders to complete initial registration before release from prison, not after.

10. The Act will require offenders to notify law enforcement within 5 days of changes in registry information.

11. The Act will require felony offenders to verify registry information in person every 6 months.

12. The Act will require juveniles who commit sex crimes against other children to register.

13. The Act will require persons convicted in foreign countries for crimes against children to register.

14. The Act will require persons convicted of possession of child pornography to register.

15. The Act will require registration information to include license plate/vehicle information and a DNA sample.

16. The Act will create a 3-year pilot program in 10 states for electronic monitoring of sex offenders.

17. The Act will require DNA samples from federal arrestees and detainees.

18. The Act will increase penalties for certain crimes against children.

19. The Act will increase protection of children in the foster care system.

20. The Act will create a federal program of civil commitment of sexual predators pursuant to established guidelines.

CHAPTER 8:
POST-ABDUCTION STRATEGIES AND RESOURCES

IN GENERAL

If your child is missing, you have no time to lose. According to law enforcement agencies, when there has been a non-family abduction, the first three hours after a child disappears are the most critical. If the child is not found within the first three hours, their chance of survival is less than twenty percent. This chapter discusses the resources available if you find yourself in this overwhelming and distressful situation, and strategies for bringing immediate and widespread attention to your missing child's case.

CONTACT LAW ENFORCEMENT

Do not hesitate in making the "911" call, hoping that your child will "turn up." In fact, notify every law enforcement agency in your area, including the FBI. FBI agents are specially trained and skilled in handling child abduction. It is best to err on the side of caution than waste precious time.

When law enforcement officials arrive, give them a complete description of your child, including their hair and eye color; height and weight; any distinguishing characteristics, e.g., eyeglasses, birth marks, etc. Describe the clothing they were wearing before they disappeared. Also, give them a color photograph that clearly depicts your child's face. If you prepared a child identification kit, as discussed in Chapter 1, provide law enforcement officials with your child's fingerprint card and/or a DNA sample. Request an AMBER Alert and ask that your child's information be entered into the National Crime Information Computer immediately.

Do not allow people to walk through your house and yard until law enforcement has conducted a proper investigation. You must preserve the crime scene so as not to disturb potentially important evidence that may lead to your child's recovery, such as fingerprints that may identify the abductor.

Cooperate fully with the investigation and answer all questions. Do not take offense if law enforcement officers appear to focus on you or your family members, even if you are asked to take a lie detector test. Your cooperation will help to eliminate you as a suspect. Such an interrogation may seem cruel at a time when you and your family are likely experiencing emotional trauma, however, it is necessary, and it will help law enforcement officers focus their attention in the right direction.

Remember, the officers don't know you personally and, in most kidnappings, the abductor is usually a family member or acquaintance of the family. Based on those statistics, law enforcement officers generally focus their investigation on ruling out family, friends and acquaintances, while investigating registered sex offenders and—the least likely but most dangerous perpetrator—the stranger.

PRIVATE INVESTIGATORS

If you decide to hire a private investigator to assist in the search for your child, you must make sure that they are licensed in your state. Find out whether they have experience in missing children cases and the outcome in those cases. You should also check their references. Discuss their fee schedule to avoid being exploited at a time when you are most vulnerable. You want results.

MONITOR PHONE CALLS

It is important to have someone at your home monitoring telephone calls in case your child tries to contact you or the kidnapper has demands. You should also have the necessary equipment to record any incoming telephone calls. Also, make sure you have the Caller ID service on your telephone line in case the calling number can be identified.

ARRANGE A GROUND SEARCH

As soon as possible after your child is missing, arrange a ground search to cover the surrounding area. Ask family members, friends, neighbors, volunteer organizations, and law enforcement to join in the search. You should also consider hiring professional ground searchers. Their assistance may prove invaluable.

Professional ground searchers are trained in conducting a ground search and often have access to the latest technology, including night vision equipment and tracking devices. They will help direct the volunteers who are assisting in the search. In addition, they may use tracking dogs that are trained to conduct missing person searches. The dog handlers will likely want to use your child's clothing or other personal items to track his or her scent.

DISTRIBUTE FLYERS

It is important to print flyers containing all of the pertinent information concerning your child's description and the circumstances surrounding his or her disappearance. As set forth below, you can create a missing child flyer on the www.beyondmissing.com website.

You must distribute the flyer throughout your community. Blanket the area with flyers. Post copies on all public bulletin boards, and on car windshields. Send copies to hospital emergency rooms, teen centers, homeless shelters, malls, and all local establishments. Distribute copies to all areas your child is known to frequent. Engage neighbors and family members in the distribution effort.

DEALING WITH THE MEDIA

Contact television and radio stations and ask them to report the details of your child's abduction to a mass audience. That is your goal—to get the circumstances of your child's disappearance out to the public and engage them in the search for your child. Members of the media may seem insensitive at times, however, their assistance can be effective.

Ask your media contacts to arrange for a press conference where you can get the message out to the community and, at the same time, make an appeal to the abductor to return your child. Provide your media contacts with photographs and videos of your child, which are an effective tool in gaining public interest in your cause. Arrange a candlelight vigil and ask that the media cover the event.

KEEP YOUR MISSING CHILD IN THE NEWS

As time goes on, the public tends to forget and the media loses interest in the story about your child. You should make every effort to keep your missing child in the news. Plan fundraisers that will attract media attention and issue press releases before and after the event. Offer a reward for information leading to your child's recovery. If there are any new developments, notify the news outlets immediately.

MISSING CHILDREN POSTCARDS

Missing children postcards have been an effective tool in the recovery of missing children. According to the National Center for Missing and Exploited Children, one in six of the missing children whose pictures are featured on these cards are recovered as a direct result of the photograph. The postcards are distributed through the mail to over 79 million homes every week.

RESOURCES

There are many resources available to assist parents whose children have suddenly disappeared, whether the child was lost or ran away; kidnapped by a parent in a custody battle; or abducted by a stranger.

Beyond Missing

Beyond Missing is a non-profit corporation dedicated to the recovery of abducted and missing children by providing high speed, cost effective communication tools to law enforcement and the communities they serve. On the Beyond Missing website, you can create and print a "missing child" flyer for duplication at no cost. In addition, law registered law enforcement agencies working on your child's case can go to the website and create and distribute flyers to other law enforcement agencies over the Internet.

For further information, contact Beyond Missing at (415) 461-FIND or (415) 461-3463 or you can visit their website at www.beyondmissing.com.

The Carole Sund/Carrington Memorial Reward Foundation

The Carole Sund/Carrington Memorial Reward Foundation is a non-profit organization that assists families with limited financial resources by offering rewards of up to $10,000 to help recover missing loved ones and to bring violent criminals to justice.

To qualify for a reward, the following criteria must be met:

The investigating agency must sanction the reward request and qualify the legitimate need.

Rewards are offered for at-risk missing person's cases, not those involving runaway or custody issues.

For further information, contact the Carole Sund/Carrington Memorial Reward Foundation at 1-888-813-8389 or visit their website at www.carolesundfoundation.com.

Child Locator Services

Every state has a nonprofit organization designated as a child locator service that specializes in the recovery of missing children. Depending on the state, their services may vary, but generally include assistance in locating missing children, preventing child abduction, resolving incidents of parental abduction through mediation. In addition, they act as a liaison among the parents of the missing child, law enforcement authorities and the media. They specialize in the recovery of missing children.

A directory of non-profit child locator organizations is set forth at Appendix 19.

State Missing Children Clearinghouses

Every state has established an agency program—generally known as a Missing Children Clearinghouse—that assists parents in locating and recovering their missing children. The scope and extent of each program varies, but depending on the state, their services may include statewide photo dissemination; assistance in obtaining state agency records and files; assistance in having your child entered into the FBI National Crime Information-Missing Person File; law enforcement training programs; and technical assistance on case investigations. You should contact your state missing children clearinghouse to find out what services it can provide in your case.

A directory of State Missing Children Clearinghouses is set forth at Appendix 20.

The National Center For Missing & Exploited Children

The National Center for Missing & Exploited Children (NCMEC) is a nonprofit organization established in 1984. Its mission is to help prevent child abduction and sexual exploitation, help find missing children, and assist victims of child abduction and sexual exploitation. The organization has a Congressional mandate to:

1. serve as a clearinghouse of information about missing and exploited children;

2. operate a CyberTipline that the public may use to report Internet-related child sexual exploitation;

3. provide technical assistance to individuals and law-enforcement agencies in the prevention, investigation, prosecution, and treatment of cases involving missing and exploited children;

4. assist the U.S. Department of State in certain cases of international child abduction in accordance with the Hague Convention on the Civil Aspects of International Child Abduction;

5. offer training programs to law-enforcement and social-service professionals;

6. distribute photographs and descriptions of missing children worldwide;

7. coordinate child-protection efforts with the private sector;

8. network with nonprofit service providers and state clearinghouses about missing-persons cases; and

9. provide information about effective state legislation to help ensure the protection of children.

For further information, contact the National Center For Missing & Exploited Children at 1-800-THE-LOST or (800) 843-5678 or visit their website at www.missingkids.com.

The National Runaway Switchboard

The National Runaway Switchboard is a federally designated national communication system for runaway and homeless children. Its mission is to keep at-risk youth safe and off the streets. Through its hotline, it assists children and their family members in resolving problems and finding help, such as finding shelter, food, medical assistance or counseling.

For further information, contact the National Runaway Switchboard at 1-800-786-2929 or visit their website at www.1800runaway.org.

Team H.O.P.E.

Team H.O.P.E. is a parent support network for families with missing children made up of mothers, fathers, siblings and extended family members who had, or still have, a missing child. With their personal experience, Team H.O.P.E. is able to uniquely provide emotional support for parents whose children are victims of predatory kidnapping, parental abduction, international abduction, and runaways.

For further information, contact Team H.O.P.E. at 1-800-306-6311 or visit their website at www.teamhope.org.

APPENDIX 1:
TABLE OF STATE MISSING CHILDREN STATUTES

STATE	STATUTE
Alabama	Code of Alabama § 26-19-1 et. seq.
Alaska	Alaska Statutes § 14.30.700 et. seq.
Arizona	Arizona Revised Statutes Annotated § 15-829
Arkansas	Arkansas Statutes Annotated § 12-12-205 et. seq.
California	California Statutes § 49068.5 et. seq.
Colorado	§ Colorado Revised Statutes § 24-33.5-415.7 et. seq.
Connecticut	Connecticut General Statutes Annotated § 29-1e et. seq.
Delaware	Delaware Code Annotated § 8531 et. seq.
District of Columbia	District of Columbia Code § 16-4603.01 et. seq.
Florida	Florida Statutes Annotated § 39.202 et. seq.
Georgia	Code of Georgia § 35-3-80 et. seq.
Hawaii	Hawaii Revised Statutes § 28-121
Idaho	Idaho Labor Code § 18-4507 et. seq.
Illinois	Illinois Revised Statutes § 2605-480 et. seq.
Indiana	Indiana Code Annotated § 10-13-5-1 et. seq.
Iowa	Code of Iowa § 694.1 et. seq.
Kansas	Kansas Statutes Annotated § 16-175 et. seq.
Kentucky	Kentucky Revised Statutes § 531.300 et. seq.
Louisiana	Louisiana Revised Statutes § 2511 et. seq.
Maine	Maine Revised Statutes Annotated § 2152 et. seq.
Maryland	2004 Md. Laws 528
Massachusetts	Massachusetts Annotated Laws Chapter 22A § 1 et. seq.

STATE	STATUTE
Michigan	Michigan Statutes Annotated § 28.258
Minnesota	Minnesota Statutes Annotated § 299C.51 et. seq.
Mississippi	Mississippi Code Annotated § 43-21-255 et. seq.
Missouri	Annotated Missouri Statutes § 210.1012 et. seq.
Montana	Revised Montana Code Annotated § 44-2-501 et. seq.
Nebraska	Nebraska Revised Statutes § 29-212 et. seq.
Nevada	Nevada Revised Statutes § 432-150 et. seq.
New Hampshire	New Hampshire Revised Statutes Annotated § 169-E:1 et. seq.
New Jersey	New Jersey Revised Statutes Annotated § 52:17B-194.1 et. seq.
New Mexico	New Mexico Statutes Annotated § 29-15A-1 et. seq.
New York	New York Executive Law § 837-e
North Carolina	General Statutes of North Carolina § 243B-495 et. seq.
North Dakota	North Dakota Century Code § 54-23.2-04.1
Ohio	Ohio Revised Code Annotated § 2901.30 et. seq.
Oklahoma	Oklahoma Statutes Annotated § 1-323.1
Oregon	Oregon Revised Statutes §181.505 et. seq.
Pennsylvania	Pennsylvania Consolidated Statutes § 2908
Rhode Island	Rhode Island General Laws § 42-28-3.1 et. seq.
South Carolina	South Carolina Code Annotated §23-3-200 et. seq.
South Dakota	South Dakota Revised Statutes § 22-19-14
Tennessee	Tennessee Code Annotated §37-10-201 et. seq.
Texas	Texas Revised Statutes § 411.351 et. seq.
Utah	Utah Code Annotated § 53-10-102
Vermont	Virginia Statutes Annotated § 1820 et. seq.
Virginia	Code of Virginia Annotated § 52-34.1 et. seq.
Washington	Washington Revised Code § 13.60.010 et. seq.
West Virginia	West Virginia Code § 49-9-1 et. seq.
Wisconsin	Wisconsin Statutes Annotated § 822.01 et. seq.
Wyoming	None – defers to federal and international laws

APPENDIX 2:
TABLE OF REGISTERED SEX OFFENDERS BY STATE

STATE	NUMBER OF REGISTERED SEX OFFENDERS
Alabama	5,619
Alaska	2,000
Arizona	14,000
Arkansas	5,878
California	103,990
Colorado	8,409
Connecticut	3,785
Delaware	3,000
District of Columbia	621
Florida	34,531
Georgia	9,682
Hawaii	2,000
Idaho	2,671
Illinois	17,100
Indiana	7,960
Iowa	6,590
Kansas	3,757
Kentucky	5,427
Louisiana	6,611
Maine	1,617
Maryland	4,308
Massachusetts	16,500
Michigan	37,134
Minnesota	16,445

STATE	NUMBER OF REGISTERED SEX OFFENDERS
Mississippi	3,411
Missouri	10,837
Montana	5,097
Nebraska	2,042
Nevada	9,718
New Hampshire	3,151
New Jersey	10,443
New Mexico	1,802
New York	21,021
North Carolina	10,864
North Dakota	876
Ohio	13,778
Oklahoma	7,711
Oregon	16,251
Pennsylvania	7,370
Rhode Island	1,500
South Carolina	8,217
South Dakota	1,710
Tennessee	8,168
Texas	38,627
Utah	8,182
Vermont	2,229
Virginia	11,873
Washington	18,631
West Virginia	2,236
Wisconsin	17,502
Wyoming	924
Total:	563,806

Source: National Center for Missing & Exploited Children

APPENDIX 3:
THE JACOB WETTERLING ACT
(42 U.S.C. § 14071)

§ 14071. JACOB WETTERLING CRIMES AGAINST CHILDREN AND SEXUALLY VIOLENT OFFENDER REGISTRATION PROGRAM

(a) In general

(1) State guidelines

The Attorney General shall establish guidelines for State programs that require—

    (A) a person who is convicted of a criminal offense against a victim who is a minor or who is convicted of a sexually violent offense to register a current address for the time period specified in subparagraph (A) of subsection (b)(6) of this section; and

    (B) a person who is a sexually violent predator to register a current address unless such requirement is terminated under subparagraph (B) of subsection (b)(6) of this section.

(2) Determination of sexually violent predator status; waiver; alternative measures—

    (A) In general

A determination of whether a person is a sexually violent predator for purposes of this section shall be made by a court after considering the recommendation of a board composed of experts in the behavior and treatment of sex offenders, victims' rights advocates, and representatives of law enforcement agencies.

    (B) Waiver

The Attorney General may waive the requirements of subparagraph (A) if the Attorney General determines that the State has established alternative procedures or legal standards for designating a person as a sexually violent predator.

alternative procedures or legal standards for designating a person as a sexually violent predator.

(C) Alternative measures

The Attorney General may also approve alternative measures of comparable or greater effectiveness in protecting the public from unusually dangerous or recidivistic sexual offenders in lieu of the specific measures set forth in this section regarding sexually violent predators.

(3) Definitions

For purposes of this section:

(A) The term "criminal offense against a victim who is a minor" means any criminal offense in a range of offenses specified by State law which is comparable to or which exceeds the following range of offenses:

(i) kidnapping of a minor, except by a parent;

(ii) false imprisonment of a minor, except by a parent;

(iii) criminal sexual conduct toward a minor;

(iv) solicitation of a minor to engage in sexual conduct;

(v) use of a minor in a sexual performance;

(vi) solicitation of a minor to practice prostitution;

(vii) any conduct that by its nature is a sexual offense against a minor;

(viii) production or distribution of child pornography, as described in section 2252, 2252, or 2252A of title 18; or

(ix) an attempt to commit an offense described in any of clauses (i) through (vii), if the State—

(I) makes such an attempt a criminal offense; and

(II) chooses to include such an offense in those which are criminal offenses against a victim who is a minor for the purposes of this section.

For purposes of this subparagraph conduct which is criminal only because of the age of the victim shall not be considered a criminal offense if the perpetrator is 18 years of age or younger.

(B) The term "sexually violent offense" means any criminal offense in a range of offenses specified by State law which is comparable to or which exceeds the range of offenses encompassed by aggravated sexual abuse or sexual abuse (as described in sections 2241 and 2242 of title 18 or as described in the State criminal code) or an offense that has as its elements engaging in physical contact with another person with intent to commit aggravated sexual abuse or sexual abuse (as described in such sections of title 18 or as described in the State criminal code).

(C) The term "sexually violent predator" means a person who has been convicted of a sexually violent offense and who suffers from a mental abnormality or personality disorder that makes the person likely to engage in predatory sexually violent offenses.

(D) The term "mental abnormality" means a congenital or acquired condition of a person that affects the emotional or volitional capacity of the person in a manner that predisposes that person to the commission of criminal sexual acts to a degree that makes the person a menace to the health and safety of other persons.

(E) The term "predatory" means an act directed at a stranger, or a person with whom a relationship has been established or promoted for the primary purpose of victimization.

(F) The term "employed, carries on a vocation" includes employment that is full-time or part-time for a period of time exceeding 14 days or for an aggregate period of time exceeding 30 days during any calendar year, whether financially compensated, volunteered, or for the purpose of government or educational benefit.

(G) The term "student" means a person who is enrolled on a full-time or part-time basis, in any public or private educational institution, including any secondary school, trade, or professional institution, or institution of higher education.

(b) Registration requirement upon release, parole, supervised release, or probation

An approved State registration program established under this section shall contain the following elements:

(1) Duties of responsible officials

(A) If a person who is required to register under this section is released from prison, or placed on parole, supervised release, or probation, a State prison officer, the court, or another responsible officer or official, shall—

(i) inform the person of the duty to register and obtain the information required for such registration;

(ii) inform the person that if the person changes residence address, the person shall report the change of address as provided by State law;

(iii) inform the person that if the person changes residence to another State, the person shall report the change of address as provided by State law and comply with any registration requirement in the new State of residence, and inform the person that the person must also register in a State where the person is employed, carries on a vocation, or is a student;

(iv) obtain fingerprints and a photograph of the person if these have not already been obtained in connection with the offense that triggers registration; and

(v) require the person to read and sign a form stating that the duty of the person to register under this section has been explained.

(B) In addition to the requirements of subparagraph (A), for a person required to register under subparagraph (B) of subsection (a)(1) of this section, the State prison officer, the court, or another responsible officer or official, as the case may be, shall obtain the name of the person, identifying factors, anticipated future residence, offense history, and documentation of any treatment received for the mental abnormality or personality disorder of the person.

(2) Transfer of information to State and FBI; participation in national sex offender registry

(A) State reporting

State procedures shall ensure that the registration information is promptly made available to a law enforcement agency having jurisdiction where the person expects to reside and entered into the appropriate State records or data system. State procedures shall also ensure that conviction data and fingerprints for persons required to register are promptly transmitted to the Federal Bureau of Investigation.

(B) National reporting

A State shall participate in the national database established under section 14072(b) of this title in accordance with guidelines issued by the Attorney General, including transmission of current address information and other information on registrants to the extent provided by the guidelines.

(3) Verification

(A) For a person required to register under subparagraph (A) of subsection (a)(1) of this section, State procedures shall provide for verification of address at least annually.

(B) The provisions of subparagraph (A) shall be applied to a person required to register under subparagraph (B) of subsection (a)(1) of this section, except that such person must verify the registration every 90 days after the date of the initial release or commencement of parole.

(4) Notification of local law enforcement agencies of changes in address

A change of address by a person required to register under this section shall be reported by the person in the manner provided by State law. State procedures shall ensure that the updated address information is promptly made available to a law enforcement agency having jurisdiction where the person will reside and entered into the appropriate State records or data system.

(5) Registration for change of address to another State

A person who has been convicted of an offense which requires registration under this section and who moves to another State, shall report the change of address to the responsible agency in the State the person is leaving, and shall comply with any registration requirement in the new State of residence. The procedures of the State the person is leaving shall ensure that notice is provided promptly to an agency responsible for registration in the new State, if that State requires registration.

(6) Length of registration

A person required to register under subsection (a)(1) of this section shall continue to comply with this section, except during ensuing periods of incarceration, until—

(A) 10 years have elapsed since the person was released from prison or placed on parole, supervised release, or probation; or

(B) For the life of that person if that person—

(i) has 1 or more prior convictions for an offense described in subsection (a)(1)(A) of this section; or

(ii) has been convicted of an aggravated offense described in subsection (a)(1)(A) of this section; or

(iii) has been determined to be a sexually violent predator pursuant to subsection (a)(2) of this section.

(7) Registration of out-of-State offenders, Federal offenders, persons sentenced by courts martial, and offenders crossing State borders

As provided in guidelines issued by the Attorney General, each State shall include in its registration program residents who were convicted in another State and shall ensure that procedures are in place to accept registration information from—

(A) residents who were convicted in another State, convicted of a Federal offense, or sentenced by a court martial; and

(B) nonresident offenders who have crossed into another State in order to work or attend school.

(c) Registration of offender crossing State border

Any person who is required under this section to register in the State in which such person resides shall also register in any State in which the person is employed, carries on a vocation, or is a student.

(d) Penalty

A person required to register under a State program established pursuant to this section who knowingly fails to so register and keep such registration current shall be subject to criminal penalties in any State in which the person has so failed.

(e) Release of information

(1) The information collected under a State registration program may be disclosed for any purpose permitted under the laws of the State.

(2) The State or any agency authorized by the State shall release relevant information that is necessary to protect the public concerning a specific person required to register under this section, except that the identity of a victim of an offense that requires registration under this section shall not be released. The release of information under this paragraph shall include the maintenance of an Internet site containing such information that is available to the public and instructions on the process for correcting information that a person alleges to be erroneous.

(f) Immunity for good faith conduct

Law enforcement agencies, employees of law enforcement agencies and independent contractors acting at the direction of such agencies, and State officials shall be immune from liability for good faith conduct under this section.

(g) Compliance

(1) Compliance date

Each State shall have not more than 3 years from September 13, 1994, in which to implement this section, except that the Attorney General may grant an additional 2 years to a State that is making good faith efforts to implement this section.

(2) Ineligibility for funds

(A) A State that fails to implement the program as described in this section shall not receive 10 percent of the funds that would otherwise be allocated to the State under section 3756 of this title.

(B) Reallocation of funds.— Any funds that are not allocated for failure to comply with this section shall be reallocated to States that comply with this section.

(h) Fingerprints

Each requirement to register under this section shall be deemed to also require the submission of a set of fingerprints of the person required to register, obtained in accordance with regulations prescribed by the Attorney General under section 14072(b) of this title.

(i) Grants to States for costs of compliance

(1) Program authorized

(A) In general

The Director of the Bureau of Justice Assistance (in this subsection referred to as the "Director") shall carry out a program, which shall be known as the "Sex Offender Management Assistance Program" (in this subsection referred to as the "SOMA program"), under which the Director shall award a grant to each eligible State to offset costs directly associated with complying with this section.

(B) Uses of funds

Each grant awarded under this subsection shall be—

(i) distributed directly to the State for distribution to State and local entities; and

(ii) used for training, salaries, equipment, materials, and other costs directly associated with complying with this section.

(2) Eligibility

(A) Application

To be eligible to receive a grant under this subsection, the chief executive of a State shall, on an annual basis, submit to the Director an application (in such form and containing such information as the Director may reasonably require) assuring that—

(i) the State complies with (or made a good faith effort to comply with) this section; and

(ii) where applicable, the State has penalties comparable to or greater than Federal penalties for crimes listed in this section, except that the Director may waive the requirement of this clause if a State demonstrates an overriding need for assistance under this subsection.

(B) Regulations

(i) In general

Not later than 90 days after October 30, 1998, the Director shall promulgate regulations to implement this subsection (including the information that must be included and the requirements that the States must meet) in submitting the applications required under this subsection. In allocating funds under this subsection, the Director may consider the annual number of sex offenders registered in each eligible State's monitoring and notification programs.

(ii) Certain training programs

Prior to implementing this subsection, the Director shall study the feasibility of incorporating into the SOMA program the activities of any technical assistance or training program established as a result of section 13941 of this title. In a case in which incorporating such activities into the SOMA program will eliminate duplication of efforts or administrative costs, the Director shall take administrative actions, as allowable, and make recommendations to Congress to incorporate such activities into the SOMA program prior to implementing the SOMA program.

(3) Authorization of appropriations

There is authorized to be appropriated for each of the fiscal years 2004 through 2007 such sums as may be necessary to carry out the provisions of section 3796dd(d)(10) of this title, as added by the PROTECT Act.

(j) Notice of enrollment at or employment by institutions of higher education

(1) Notice by offenders

(A) In general

In addition to any other requirements of this section, any person who is required to register in a State shall provide notice as required under State law—

(i) of each institution of higher education in that State at which the person is employed, carries on a vocation, or is a student; and

(ii) of each change in enrollment or employment status of such person at an institution of higher education in that State.

(B) Change in status

A change in status under subparagraph (A)(ii) shall be reported by the person in the manner provided by State law. State procedures shall ensure that the updated information is promptly made available to a law enforcement agency having jurisdiction where such institution is located and entered into the appropriate State records or data system.

(2) State reporting

State procedures shall ensure that the registration information collected under paragraph (1)—

(A) is promptly made available to a law enforcement agency having jurisdiction where such institution is located; and

(B) entered into the appropriate State records or data system.

(3) Request

Nothing in this subsection shall require an educational institution to request such information from any State.

§ 14072. FBI DATABASE

(a) Definitions

For purposes of this section—

(1) the term "FBI" means the Federal Bureau of Investigation;

(2) the terms "criminal offense against a victim who is a minor", "sexually violent offense", "sexually violent predator", "mental abnormality", "predatory", "employed, carries on a vocation", and "student" have the same meanings as in section 14071 (a)(3) of this title; and

(3) the term "minimally sufficient sexual offender registration program" means any State sexual offender registration program that—

(A) requires the registration of each offender who is convicted of an offense in a range of offenses specified by State law which is comparable to or exceeds that described in subparagraph (A) or (B) of section 14071 (a)(1) of this title;

(B) participates in the national database established under subsection (b) of this section in conformity with guidelines issued by the Attorney General;

(C) provides for verification of address at least annually; [and]

(D) requires that each person who is required to register under subparagraph (A) shall do so for a period of not less than 10 years beginning on the date that such person was released from prison or placed on parole, supervised release, or probation.

(b) Establishment

The Attorney General shall establish a national database at the Federal Bureau of Investigation to track the whereabouts and movement of—

(1) each person who has been convicted of a criminal offense against a victim who is a minor;

(2) each person who has been convicted of a sexually violent offense; and

(3) each person who is a sexually violent predator.

(c) Registration requirement

Each person described in subsection (b) of this section who resides in a State that has not established a minimally sufficient sexual offender registration program shall register a current address, fingerprints of that person, and a current photograph of that person with the FBI for inclusion in the database established under subsection (b) of this section for the time period specified under subsection (d) of this section.

(d) Length of registration

A person described in subsection (b) of this section who is required to register under subsection (c) of this section shall, except during ensuing periods of incarceration, continue to comply with this section—

(1) until 10 years after the date on which the person was released from prison or placed on parole, supervised release, or probation; or

(2) for the life of the person, if that person—

(A) has 2 or more convictions for an offense described in subsection (b) of this section;

(B) has been convicted of aggravated sexual abuse, as defined in section 2241 of title 18 or in a comparable provision of State law; or

(C) has been determined to be a sexually violent predator.

(e) Verification

(1) Persons convicted of an offense against a minor or a sexually violent offense

In the case of a person required to register under subsection (c) of this section, the FBI shall, during the period in which the person is required to register under subsection (d) of this section, verify the person's address in accordance with guidelines that shall be promulgated by the Attorney General. Such guidelines shall ensure that address verification is accomplished with respect to these individuals and shall require the submission of fingerprints and photographs of the individual.

(2) Sexually violent predators

Paragraph (1) shall apply to a person described in subsection (b)(3) of this section, except that such person must verify the registration once every 90 days after the date of the initial release or commencement of parole of that person.

(f) Community notification

(1) In general

Subject to paragraph (2), the FBI may release relevant information concerning a person required to register under subsection (c) of this section that is necessary to protect the public.

(2) Identity of victim

In no case shall the FBI release the identity of any victim of an offense that requires registration by the offender with the FBI.

(g) Notification of FBI of changes in residence

(1) Establishment of new residence

For purposes of this section, a person shall be deemed to have established a new residence during any period in which that person resides for not less than 10 days.

(2) Persons required to register with the FBI

Each establishment of a new residence, including the initial establishment of a residence immediately following release from prison, or placement on parole, supervised release, or probation, by a person required to register under subsection (c) of this section shall be reported to the FBI not later than 10 days after that person establishes a new residence.

(3) Individual registration requirement

A person required to register under subsection (c) of this section or under a State sexual offender registration program, including a program established under section 14071 of this title, who changes address to a State other than the State in which the person resided at the time of the immediately preceding registration shall, not later than 10 days after that person establishes a new residence, register a current address, fingerprints, and photograph of that person, for inclusion in the appropriate database, with—

(A) the FBI; and

(B) the State in which the new residence is established.

(4) State registration requirement

Any time any State agency in a State with a minimally sufficient sexual offender registration program, including a program established under section 14071 of this title, is notified of a change of address by a person required to register under such program within or outside of such State, the State shall notify—

(A) the law enforcement officials of the jurisdiction to which, and the jurisdiction from which, the person has relocated; and

(B) the FBI.

(5) Verification

(A) Notification of local law enforcement officials

The FBI shall ensure that State and local law enforcement officials of the jurisdiction from which, and the State and local law enforcement officials of the jurisdiction to which, a person required to register under subsection (c) of this section relocates are notified of the new residence of such person.

(B) Notification of FBI

A State agency receiving notification under this subsection shall notify the FBI of the new residence of the offender.

(C) Verification

(i) State agencies

If a State agency cannot verify the address of or locate a person required to register with a minimally sufficient sexual offender registration program, including a program established under section 14071 of this title, the State shall immediately notify the FBI.

(ii) FBI

If the FBI cannot verify the address of or locate a person required to register under subsection (c) of this section or if the FBI receives notification from a State under clause (i), the FBI shall—

(I) classify the person as being in violation of the registration requirements of the national database; and

(II) add the name of the person to the National Crime Information Center Wanted person file and create a wanted persons record: Provided, That an arrest warrant which meets the requirements for entry into the file is issued in connection with the violation.

(h) Fingerprints

(1) FBI registration

For each person required to register under subsection (c) of this section, fingerprints shall be obtained and verified by the FBI or a local law enforcement official pursuant to regulations issued by the Attorney General.

(2) State registration systems

In a State that has a minimally sufficient sexual offender registration program, including a program established under section 14071 of this title, fingerprints required to be registered with the FBI under this section shall be obtained and verified in accordance with State requirements. The State agency responsible for registration shall ensure that the fingerprints and all other information required to be registered is registered with the FBI.

(i) Penalty

A person who is—

(1) required to register under paragraph (1), (2), or (3) of subsection (g) of this section and knowingly fails to comply with this section;

(2) required to register under a sexual offender registration program in the person's State of residence and knowingly fails to register in any other State in which the person is employed, carries on a vocation, or is a student;

(3) described in section 4042 (c)(4) of title 18, and knowingly fails to register in any State in which the person resides, is employed, carries

on a vocation, or is a student following release from prison or sentencing to probation; or

(4) sentenced by a court martial for conduct in a category specified by the Secretary of Defense under section 115(a)(8)(C) of title I of Public Law 105–119, and knowingly fails to register in any State in which the person resides, is employed, carries on a vocation, or is a student following release from prison or sentencing to probation, shall, in the case of a first offense under this subsection, be imprisoned for not more than 1 year and, in the case of a second or subsequent offense under this subsection, be imprisoned for not more than 10 years.

(j) Release of information

The information collected by the FBI under this section shall be disclosed by the FBI—

(1) to Federal, State, and local criminal justice agencies for—

(A) law enforcement purposes; and

(B) community notification in accordance with section 14071 (d)(3) of this title; and

(2) to Federal, State, and local governmental agencies responsible for conducting employment-related background checks under section 5119a of this title.

(k) Notification upon release

Any State not having established a program described in subsection (a)(3) of this section must—

(1) upon release from prison, or placement on parole, supervised release, or probation, notify each offender who is convicted of an offense described in subparagraph (A) or (B) of section 14701 of this title of their duty to register with the FBI; and

(2) notify the FBI of the release of each offender who is convicted of an offense described in subparagraph (A) or (B) of section 14071 (a)(1) of this title.

§ 14073. IMMUNITY FOR GOOD FAITH CONDUCT

State and Federal law enforcement agencies, employees of State and Federal law enforcement agencies, and State and Federal officials shall be immune from liability for good faith conduct under section 14072 of this title.

APPENDIX 4:
STATE SEX OFFENDER REGISTRATION WEBSITES

STATE	WEBSITE
ALABAMA	http://www.dps.state.al.us
ALASKA	http://www.dps.state.ak.us/nsorcr/asp
ARIZONA	http://www.azsexoffender.com/
ARKANSAS	http://www.acic.org/Registration/index.htm
CALIFORNIA	http://www.meganslaw.ca.gov/
COLORADO	http://sor.state.co.us/default.asp
CONNECTICUT	http://www.state.ct.us/dps
DELAWARE	http://www.state.de.us/dsp/sexoff/index.htm
DISTRICT OF COLUMBIA	http://www.mpdc.dc.gov
FLORIDA	http://www.fdle.state.fl.us/index.asp?/sexual_predators/
GEORGIA	http://www.Georgia-Sex-Offenders.com

STATE	WEBSITE
HAWAII	http://pahoehoe.ehawaii.gov/sexoff/index.html
IOWA	http://www.iowasexoffenders.com
IDAHO	http://www.isp.state.id.us/identification/sex_offender/index.html
ILLINOIS	http://www.isp.state.il.us/sor/frames.htm
INDIANA	http://www.state.in.us/serv/cji_sor
KANSAS	http://www.accesskansas.org/kbi/ro.htm
KENTUCKY	http://kspsor.state.ky.us/
LOUISIANA	http://www.lasocpr.lsp.org/socpr/
MAINE	http://www4.informe.org/sor/
MARYLAND	http://www.dpscs.state.md.us/sor/
MASSACHUSETTS	http://www.state.ma.us/sorb/community.htm
MICHIGAN	http://www.mipsor.state.mi.us
MINNESOTA	http://www.doc.state.mn.us/level3/level3.asp
MISSISSIPPI	http://www.sor.mdps.state.ms.us/
MISSOURI	http://www.mshp.dps.missouri.gov/MSHPWeb/PatrolDivisions/
MONTANA	http://www.doj.mt.gov/svor/
NEBRASKA	http://www.nsp.state.ne.us/sor/find.cfm
NEVADA	http://www.nvsexoffenders.gov
NEW HAMPSHIRE	http://oit.nh.gov/nsor/
NEW JERSEY	http://www.state.nj.us/lps/dcj/megan/meghome.htm
NEW MEXICO	http://www.nmsexoffender.dps.state.nm.us/

STATE	WEBSITE
NEW YORK	http://criminaljustice.state.ny.us/nsor/index.htm
NORTH CAROLINA	http://sbi.jus.state.nc.us/DOJHAHT/SOR/default.htm
NORTH DAKOTA	http://www.ndsexoffender.com
OHIO	http://www.ag.state.oh.us
OKLAHOMA	http://docapp8.doc.state.ok.us
OREGON	http://www.co.benton.or.us/sheriff/corrections/bccc/sonote/
PENNSYLVANIA	http://www.psp.state.pa.us
SOUTH CAROLINA	http://www.sled.state.sc.us
SOUTH DAKOTA	http://www.sddci.com/administration/id/sexoffender/index.asp
TENNESSEE	http://www.ticic.state.tn.us/
TEXAS	http://records.txdps.state.tx.us/
UTAH	http://corrections.utah.gov/community/sexoffenders/ Email: registry@udc.state.ut.us
VERMONT	http://www.dps.state.vt.us/cjs/s_registry.htm (Information only)
VIRGINIA	http://sex-offender.vsp.state.va.us/cool-ICE/
WASHINGTON	http://ml.waspc.org
WEST VIRGINIA	http://www.wvstatepolice.com
WISCONSIN	http://offender.doc.state.wi.us/public/
WYOMING	http://attorneygeneral.state.wy.us/dci/so/so_registration.html

APPENDIX 5:
STATE AMBER ALERT CONTACTS

STATE	CONTACT	TELEPHONE	WEBSITE
ALABAMA	Alabama Bureau of Investigation	800-228-7688	http://www.dps.state.al.us/public/abi/amber_plan.asp
ALASKA	Alaska State Troopers	907-269-5413	none listed
ARIZONA	Arizona Broadcasters Association	602-252-4833	none listed
ARKANSAS	Arkansas State Police	501-618-8803	http://www.todaysthv.com/community/morgannick/default.asp
CALIFORNIA	California Highway Patrol	916-227-6388	http://www.chp.ca.gov/html/amber-en.html
COLORADO	Colorado Bureau of Investigation	303-239-4251	http://www.cbi.state.co.us/mp/amber/amberlist.asp
CONNECTICUT	Connecticut State Police	860-685-8032	http://www.state.ct.us/dps/Amber_Alert.htm

STATE	CONTACT	TELEPHONE	WEBSITE
DELAWARE	Delaware State Police	302-834-2620,	http://www.state.de.us/governor/news/2003/01january/011403%20-%20amber%20alert%20implementation.shtml
DISTRICT OF COLUMBIA	none listed	none listed	http://www.dcamberplan.com/
FLORIDA	Florida Department of Law Enforcement	888-356-4774	http://www.fdle.state.fl.us/AmberPlan/
GEORGIA	Georgia Bureau of Investigation	404-244-2550	none listed
HAWAII	Hawaii Missing Children's Clearinghouse	808-586-1449	none listed
IDAHO	Idaho Bureau of Homeland Security	208-334-3460	http://www2.state.id.us/gcc/newsletter/9.06.03.htm
ILLINOIS	Illinois State Police	800-843-5763	http://www.isp.state.il.us/crime/amber.htm
INDIANA	Indiana State Police	317-232-8200	http://www.amberalertindiana.com/
IOWA	none listed	none listed	http://www.iowaamberalert.com
KANSAS	Kansas Attorney General's Office	785-296-2215	http://www.ksamber.org/
KENTUCKY	Kentucky State Police	502-227-2221	none listed
LOUISIANA	Louisiana State Police	225-925-6325	http://www.lsp.org/amber.html
MARYLAND	Maryland Center for Missing Children	800-637 5437	http://www.mdamberplan.com/
MICHIGAN	Michigan State Police	517-333-4017	http://www.michigan.gov/msp/0,1607,7-123—19738—,00.html

STATE	CONTACT	TELEPHONE	WEBSITE
MINNESOTA	Minnesota Crime Alert Network	651-642-0779	http://www.dps.state.mn.us/mcan/AmberAlert/index.htm
MISSISSIPPI	Mississippi Highway Patrol	601-987-1390	http://www.dps.state.ms.us/dps/dps.nsf/divpages/ci3amber?OpenDocument
MISSOURI	Missouri Department of Public Safety	573-751- 4905	http://www.dps.state.mo.us/home/AbductionForm.htm
MONTANA	Montana Missing Person Clearinghouse	406-444-1526	http://www.doj.state.mt.us/enforcement/missingpersonclearinghouse.asp
NEBRASKA	Nebraska State Patrol	none listed	www.nsp.state.ne.us
NEVADA	State of Nevada Office of the Attorney General	702-486-3107	http://amberalert.nv.gov/
NEW HAMPSHIRE	New Hampshire State Police	603-271 2663	none listed
NEW JERSEY	New Jersey State Police	609-882-2000	http://www.njsp.org/amber/
NEW YORK	New York State Police	518-457-8678	http://nysamber.troopers.state.ny.us/
NORTH CAROLINA	North Carolina Center for Missing Persons	800-522-5437	none listed
NORTH DAKOTA	North Dakota State Patrol	701-328-2455	http://www.state.nd.us/amber/
OHIO	Ohio Missing Children Clearinghouse	800-325-5604	http://www.ohioamberplan.org/
OKLAHOMA	Office of Governor Brad Henry	405-521-2342	none listed
OREGON	Oregon State Police - Bureau of Investigation	503-378-3725,	http://www.portlandonline.com/index.cfm?&a=bjfad&c=cggfj

STATE	CONTACT	TELEPHONE	WEBSITE
PENNSYLVANIA	Pennsylvania State Police	717-783-0960	http://www.amber.state.pa.us/amber/site/default.asp
RHODE ISLAND	Rhode Island State Police	401-444-1000	http://www.risp.state.ri.us/amber.php
SOUTH CAROLINA	South Carolina Law Enforcement Division (SLED)	803-896-7008	www.sled.state.sc.us
SOUTH DAKOTA	none listed	none listed	http://www.state.sd.us/amberalert/
TENNESSEE	Tennessee Bureau of Investigation	615-744-4000	www.tbi.state.tn.us
TEXAS	Texas Department of Public Safety	512-424-2208	http://www.governor.state.tx.us/divisions/press/initiatives/amber
UTAH	State of Utah Office of the Attorney General	none listed	http://www.attorneygeneral.utah.gov/AL/amberalert.htm
VERMONT	Vermont State Police	802-244-8727	www.vtsp.org/amber
VIRGINIA	Virginia State Police	804-674-2023	www.vaambera;ert/cp,
WASHINGTON	Washington State Patrol	360-753-5299	http://www.wsp.wa.gov/missing/faqmiss.htm
WEST VIRGINIA	West Virginia State Police	none listed	www.wvstatepolice.com
WISCONSIN	Wisconsin Clearinghouse for Missing & Exploited Children	none listed	none listed
WYOMING	Wyoming Office of the Attorney General	307-777-7537	none listed

APPENDIX 6:
PROTECT ACT

PUBLIC LAW 108–21 4/30/2003

SECTION 1. SHORT TITLE; TABLE OF CONTENTS.

(a) SHORT TITLE.—This Act may be cited as the "Prosecutorial Remedies and Other Tools to end the Exploitation of Children Today Act of 2003" or "PROTECT Act".

(b) TABLE OF CONTENTS.—The table of contents for this Act is as follows:

TITLE II—INVESTIGATIONS AND PROSECUTIONS

Sec. 201. Interceptions of communications in investigations of sex offenses.

Sec. 202. No statute of limitations for child abduction and sex crimes.

Sec. 203. No pretrial release for those who rape or kidnap children.

Sec. 204. Suzanne's law.

TITLE III—PUBLIC OUTREACH

SUBTITLE A—AMBER Alert

Sec. 301. National coordination of AMBER alert communications network.

Sec. 302. Minimum standards for issuance and dissemination of alerts through AMBER alert communications network.

Sec. 303. Grant program for notification and communications systems along highways for recovery of abducted children.

Sec. 304. Grant program for support of AMBER alert communications plans.

Sec. 305. Limitation on liability.

SUBTITLE B—National Center for Missing and Exploited Children

Sec. 321. Increased support.

Sec. 322. Forensic and investigative support of missing and exploited children.

Sec. 323. Creation of cybertipline.

SUBTITLE C—Sex Offender Apprehension Program

Sec. 341. Authorization.

SUBTITLE D—Missing Children Procedures in Public Buildings

Sec. 361. SHORT TITLE.

* * *

TITLE III—PUBLIC OUTREACH

SUBTITLE A—AMBER Alert

SEC. 301. NATIONAL COORDINATION OF AMBER ALERT COMMUNICATIONS NETWORK.

(a) COORDINATION WITHIN DEPARTMENT OF JUSTICE.—The Attorney General shall assign an officer of the Department of Justice to act as the national coordinator of the AMBER Alert communications network regarding abducted children. The officer so designated shall be known as the AMBER Alert Coordinator of the Department of Justice.

(b) DUTIES.—In acting as the national coordinator of the AMBER Alert communications network, the Coordinator shall—

(1) seek to eliminate gaps in the network, including gaps in areas of interstate travel;

(2) work with States to encourage the development of additional elements (known as local AMBER plans) in the network;

(3) work with States to ensure appropriate regional coordination of various elements of the network; and

(4) act as the nationwide point of contact for—

(A) the development of the network; and

(B) regional coordination of alerts on abducted children through the network.

(c) CONSULTATION WITH FEDERAL BUREAU OF INVESTIGATION.—In carrying out duties under subsection (b), the Coordinator shall notify and consult with the Director of the Federal Bureau of Investigation concerning each child abduction for which an alert is issued through the AMBER Alert communications network.

(d) COOPERATION.—The Coordinator shall cooperate with the Secretary of Transportation and the Federal Communications Commission in carrying out activities under this section.

(e) REPORT.—Not later than March 1, 2005, the Coordinator shall submit to Congress a report on the activities of the Coordinator and the effectiveness and status of the AMBER plans of each State that has implemented such a plan. The Coordinator shall prepare the report in consultation with the Secretary of Transportation.

SEC. 302. MINIMUM STANDARDS FOR ISSUANCE AND DISSEMINATION OF ALERTS THROUGH AMBER ALERT COMMUNICATIONS NETWORK.

(a) ESTABLISHMENT OF MINIMUM STANDARDS.—Subject to subsection (b), the AMBER Alert Coordinator of the Department of Justice shall establish minimum standards for—

(1) the issuance of alerts through the AMBER Alert communications network; and

(2) the extent of the dissemination of alerts issued through the network.

(b) LIMITATIONS.—

(1) The minimum standards established under subsection (a) shall be adoptable on a voluntary basis only.

(2) The minimum standards shall, to the maximum extent practicable (as determined by the Coordinator in consultation with State and local law enforcement agencies), provide that appropriate information relating to the special needs of an abducted child (including health care needs) are disseminated to the appropriate law enforcement, public health, and other public officials.

(3) The minimum standards shall, to the maximum extent practicable (as determined by the Coordinator in consultation with State and local law enforcement agencies), provide that the dissemination of an alert through the AMBER Alert communications network be limited to the geographic areas most likely to facilitate the recovery of the abducted child concerned.

(4) In carrying out activities under subsection (a), the Coordinator may not interfere with the current system of voluntary coordination between local broadcasters and State and local law enforcement agencies for purposes of the AMBER Alert communications network.

(c) COOPERATION.—

(1) The Coordinator shall cooperate with the Secretary of Transportation and the Federal Communications Commission in carrying out activities under this section.

(2) The Coordinator shall also cooperate with local broadcasters and State and local law enforcement agencies in establishing minimum standards under this section.

SEC. 303. GRANT PROGRAM FOR NOTIFICATION AND COMMUNICATIONS SYSTEMS ALONG HIGHWAYS FOR RECOVERY OF ABDUCTED CHILDREN.

(a) PROGRAM REQUIRED.—The Secretary of Transportation shall carry out a program to provide grants to States for the development or enhancement of notification or communications systems along highways for alerts and other information for the recovery of abducted children.

(b) DEVELOPMENT GRANTS.—

(1) IN GENERAL.—The Secretary may make a grant to a State under this subsection for the development of a State program for the use of changeable message signs or other motorist information systems to notify motorists about abductions of children. The State program shall provide for the planning, coordination, and design of systems, protocols, and message sets that support the coordination and communication necessary to notify motorists about abductions of children.

(2) ELIGIBLE ACTIVITIES.—A grant under this subsection may be used by a State for the following purposes:

(A) To develop general policies and procedures to guide the use of changeable message signs or other motorist information systems to notify motorists about abductions of children.

(B) To develop guidance or policies on the content and format of alert messages to be conveyed on changeable message signs or other traveler information systems.

(C) To coordinate State, regional, and local plans for the use of changeable message signs or other transportation related issues.

(D) To plan secure and reliable communications systems and protocols among public safety and transportation agencies or modify existing communications systems to support the notification of motorists about abductions of children.

(E) To plan and design improved systems for communicating with motorists, including the capability for issuing wide area alerts to motorists.

(F) To plan systems and protocols to facilitate the efficient issuance of child abduction notification and other key information to motorists during off-hours.

(G) To provide training and guidance to transportation authorities to facilitate appropriate use of changeable message signs and other traveler information systems for the notification of motorists about abductions of children.

(c) IMPLEMENTATION GRANTS.—

(1) IN GENERAL.—The Secretary may make a grant to a State under this subsection for the implementation of a program for the use of

changeable message signs or other motorist information systems to notify motorists about abductions of children. A State shall be eligible for a grant under this subsection if the Secretary determines that the State has developed a State program in accordance with subsection (b).

(2) ELIGIBLE ACTIVITIES.—A grant under this subsection may be used by a State to support the implementation of systems that use changeable message signs or other motorist information systems to notify motorists about abductions of children. Such support may include the purchase and installation of changeable message signs or other motorist information systems to notify motorists about abductions of children.

(d) FEDERAL SHARE.—The Federal share of the cost of any activities funded by a grant under this section may not exceed 80 percent.

(e) DISTRIBUTION OF GRANT AMOUNTS.—The Secretary shall, to the maximum extent practicable, distribute grants under this section equally among the States that apply for a grant under this section within the time period prescribed by the Secretary.

(f) ADMINISTRATION.—The Secretary shall prescribe requirements, including application requirements, for the receipt of grants under this section.

(g) DEFINITION.—In this section, the term "State" means any of the 50 States, the District of Columbia, or Puerto Rico.

(h) AUTHORIZATION OF APPROPRIATIONS.—There is authorized to be appropriated to the Secretary to carry out this section $20,000,000 for fiscal year 2004. Such amounts shall remain available until expended.

(i) STUDY OF STATE PROGRAMS.—

(1) STUDY.—The Secretary shall conduct a study to examine State barriers to the adoption and implementation of State programs for the use of communications systems along highways for alerts and other information for the recovery of abducted children.

(2) REPORT.—Not later than 1 year after the date of enactment of this Act, the Secretary shall transmit to Congress a report on the results of the study, together with any recommendations the Secretary determines appropriate.

SEC. 304. GRANT PROGRAM FOR SUPPORT OF AMBER ALERT COMMUNICATIONS PLANS.

(a) PROGRAM REQUIRED.—The Attorney General shall carry out a program to provide grants to States for the development or enhancement of programs and activities for the support of AMBER Alert communications plans.

(b) ACTIVITIES.—Activities funded by grants under the program under subsection (a) may include—

(1) the development and implementation of education and training programs, and associated materials, relating to AMBER Alert communications plans;

(2) the development and implementation of law enforcement programs, and associated equipment, relating to AMBER Alert communications plans;

(3) the development and implementation of new technologies to improve AMBER Alert communications; and

(4) such other activities as the Attorney General considers appropriate for supporting the AMBER Alert communications program.

(c) FEDERAL SHARE.—The Federal share of the cost of any activities funded by a grant under the program under subsection (a) may not exceed 50 percent.

(d) DISTRIBUTION OF GRANT AMOUNTS ON GEOGRAPHIC BASIS.—The Attorney General shall, to the maximum extent practicable, ensure the distribution of grants under the program under subsection (a) on an equitable basis throughout the various regions of the United States.

(e) ADMINISTRATION.—The Attorney General shall prescribe requirements, including application requirements, for grants under the program under subsection (a).

(f) AUTHORIZATION OF APPROPRIATIONS.—

(1) There is authorized to be appropriated for the Department of Justice $5,000,000 for fiscal year 2004 to carry out this section and, in addition, $5,000,000 for fiscal year 2004 to carry out subsection (b)(3).

(2) Amounts appropriated pursuant to the authorization of appropriations in paragraph (1) shall remain available until expended.

SEC. 305. LIMITATION ON LIABILITY.

(a) Except as provided in subsection (b), the National Center for Missing and Exploited Children, including any of its officers, employees, or agents, shall not be liable for damages in any civil action for defamation, libel, slander, or harm to reputation arising out of any action or communication by the National Center for Missing and Exploited Children, its officers, employees, or agents, in connection with any clearinghouse, hotline or complaint intake or forwarding program or in connection with activity that is wholly or partially funded by the United States and undertaken in cooperation with, or at the direction of a Federal law enforcement agency.

(b) The limitation in subsection (a) does not apply in any action in which the plaintiff proves that the National Center for Missing and Exploited Children, its officers, employees, or agents acted with actual malice, or provided information or took action for a purpose unrelated to an activity mandated by Federal law. For purposes of this subsection, the prevention, or detection of crime, and the safety, recovery, or protection of missing or exploited children shall be deemed, per se, to be an activity mandated by Federal law.

APPENDIX 7:
DIRECTORY OF CODE ADAM PARTICIPANTS

A R Financial™

A&P Group®

AAFES®

Academy® Sports & Outdoors

ADC, Inc.™

Addison (IL) Park District®

Adventure Science Museum - Nashville, TN

Aiken (SC) Police Department

Akron-Summit (OH) County Public Library

Albertson's Groceries®

Alexandria (MN) Clinic

All American Home Center - Downey, CA

Alpha Omega Protective Services - Northwood, OH

Alpha Park (IL) Public Library

American Guard Services

Amon Carter Museum - Fort Worth, TX

Anchorage (AK) Police Department

Anchorage (AK) Public Lands Information Center

Anderson (IN) Public Library

Angel Medical Center - Franklin, NC

Apartment Association of Greater Wichita (KS)

APIX™

Aquarium of the Bay - San Francisco, CA

Arizona Office of the Attorney General

Arizona Science Center

Arkansas Attorney General's Office

Art Van Furniture

Asheville's (NC) Fun Depot

Ashley Furniture Homestore®

Athletic Club of Bend (OR)

Atlantic Health System

Austin (TX) Museum of Art™

Austin Woods (OH) Healthcare

B&B Hotel™ - N Richland, TX

B&R Stores, Inc.

Baby Love Inc.- Sunrise, FL

Bachrach Clothing, Inc.

Bal Harbour (FL) City Hall

Ballston (VA) Common Mall

Banana Republic®

Baptist Children's Hospital - Miami, FL

Barnes & Noble Booksellers™

Barracks Road (VA) Shopping Center

Bartlett (IL) Public Library District

Bashas'™

Basilica of Saint Mary (MN)

Bass Pro Shops Outdoor World™

Bay (MI) Regional Medical Center

Bayshore (NJ) Community Hospital

BCI Personal Development Centers

Beaman (MA) Memorial Public Library

Beaverton (OR) City Library

Becker (MN) Furniture World

Bed Bath and Beyond®

Belk Inc.

Bella Vista (AZ) Sheriff's Office

Bellizzi Restaurant - Larchmont, NY

Bell's Nursery®

Belz Factory Outlet World - Las Vegas, NV

Ben & Ari's Family Entertainment Center - Fishers, IN

Ben Elias Industries

Bennett Lumber Products, Inc

Best Buy®

Bethel A.M.E. Church - Milwaukee, WI

Beuhler Food Markets, Inc.

Big Lots!™

Big Wheel Family Roller Skating Center

Bill Collins Ford™

BI-LO, LLC

Blain Farm & Fleet Stores

Blaisdell Center

Bloomington (IN) Hospital Warehouse

Bloomington (IN) Public Library

Bobtail Ice Cream Company

Bon Marche™

Books-A-Million

Boone (IA) County Hospital

Borders Books & Music®

Borough of Glassboro (NJ)

Boscov's Department Store, LLC

Branch Brook Company

Brandwine Hundred Library - New Castle, DE

Bread and Company - Nashville, TN

Bright Beginnings - Florence, KY

Bristol Park (CA) Medical

Broadlawns (IA) Medical Center

Buffalo Grove (IL) Park District

Bureau of Facilities Management, State of Virginia

Burger King® - Alma, MI Locations

BurkeView Hauling, Inc.™

Burlington Coat Factory Stores™

Burns Park (AR) Athletic Association

Butterfield (IL) Park District

Buttons and Bows

Byrd (LA) Regional Hospital

Cabela's®

Caccitore's Foods

Cal Skate GT - Grand Terrace, CA

Caldwell Zoo - Tyler, TX

Calgary Science Centre - Alberta, Canada

Camp Tamarancho - Fairfax, CA

Care Coalition - Selma, AL

CarMax, Inc.™

Carousel Resort Hotel & Condominiums

Cedar Park (TX) Public Library

CentraCare Clinic Women & Children

Central Christian Church (NV)

Chadwick & Trace™

Chester Lanes LLC

Chicago (IL) Museum of Science and Industry

Children's Museum of Manhattan (NY)

Children's Museum of Houston (TX)

Christ Outreach Deliverance Center - Bellwood, IL

Christ Outreach Ministries - Chicago, IL

Christmas Tree Shops, Inc.

Chuck E. Cheese™

Cincinnati (OH) Art Museum

Circuit City™

City of Coconut Creek (FL)

City of Phoenix (AZ) Police Department

Clearlake (CA) Cinema

Columbus (GA) Civic Center

Columbus (OH) Metropolitan Library

Columbus (OH) Metropolitan Library

Commonwealth of Puerto Rico Public Buildings Authority

Community Health Center of Snohomish (WA)

Cornerstone Chapel - Leesburg, VA

Cosley (IL) Zoo

Coyote Bar & Grill

Cross Country (NY) Shopping Center

Crossroads (MO) Regional Medical Center

Crossroads (TX) Mall™

Crown Coliseum - Fayetteville, NC

Crowne Plaza Hotel®

Crystal Lake (IL) Library

D & F Productions™

Daffy's

Dan's Gift Shop - Garden Grove, CA

Dave & Buster's

Deals - Crystal Lake, IL

Definitely Learning Child Care Center

Department of Homeland Security

Department of the Family (ADSEF) - San Juan, PR

Designer Stone®

Developmental and Forensic Pediatrics PA - Fayetteville, NC

Dick's Sporting Goods®

Dierbergs Markets, Inc.

Dillards

Dills Best Building Centers, Inc.

Discovery Center Museum

DKNY®

Dominicks Finer Foods -Crystal Lake, IL

Downers Grove (IL) Park District

Duckwall-Alco Stores™

Eagleton (KY) Federal Courthouse

Elements & Botanicals Ltd

Ellen's Place - Garland, TX

EMCOR®

Escambia County (FL) School District

Ethan Allen Stores®

Factory Card Outlet™

Family Chiropractic - Langhorne, PA

Family Identification Services®

Famous Footwear™

FAO Schwarz®

Federal Protective Service

FireLake Discount Foods™

First Alert Search and Rescue

First State Bank

Flandrau Science Center and Planetarium

Food Circus Supermarkets, Inc.

Food Lion LLC

Forest City Enterprises-The Mall at Robinson (PA)

Forman Mills®

Fort Worth ISD

Fortunoff®

Franco's Athletic Club

Frenchtown (MI) Square Mall™

Fry's Electronics™

Fry's Food and Drug™

Fun In Motion (F.I.M.)™

Fun Spot Skating Center - Belleville, IL

Funway USA®

G.I. Joe's, Inc. SM

G.WIZ™

Gander Mountain™ - Forest Lake, MN

Gap Inc.®

Garden Ridge, L.P.

Gaston County (NC) Health Department

Genesys (MI) Regional Medical Center

Gertrude Ford Center for the Performing Arts

Giant Eagle®

Gibson General Hospital

Gilbert (AZ) Police Department

Goodwill Stores

Google Inc.™

Gordman's Department Store™

Gordmans

Gordy's True Value®

Grapevine Surgicare

Greene Memorial Hospital - Xenia, OH

Greentree (PA) Sportsplex

Grotto Pizza - Nassau, DE

Guardone Security®

Half Price Books®

Hamilton (CN) Health Sciences

Hampton Bays (NY) Public Library

Hangin' Outback with Dingo and Friends

Hannaford Bros.®

Hannaford Shop and Save Supermarkets™

Happy Joe's Restaurant

Harmons City Inc

Harps Food Stores, Inc.

Hatton Industries Securities™

Hawaii Attorney General's Office

Healthbridge Fitness Center

Heavenly Air™

Heinen's Fine Foods

HelpMate Services, Inc

HH Greg Appliances, Inc

Hidalgo (TX) Police Department

Hobby Lobby®

Home Depot®

HRC™

Hugo's Grocery Stores

Iceland Arena

Ident-A-Kid of Mississippi, Inc.

IGA Marketplace®

Illinois Department of Natural Resources

Imaginarium™

Indianapolis (IN) Museum of Art

Ingles Markets, Inc.™

Intradeco Inc

J.C. Penney™

J.P. Igloo - Ellenton, FL

Jacobson's - Winterpark, FL

Jeff Anderson Regional Medical Center - Meridian, MI

Jewel-Osco®

Jewish Community Center of Greater Kansas City (KS)

Jillian's Entertainment™

Jody's Music Center - Richmond, VA

Joseph-Beth Booksellers - Pittsburgh, PA

Kaiyou Shin Kai Karate School®

KB Toys™

Kenema (MD) District Association

Kennewick (WA) General Hospital

Kids Furniture Factory™

KidSenses Children's InterActive Museum™

Kidz Kare Enterprise

Kindred Hospital - Dayton, OH

Kirschman's®

Klamath County (OR) Sheriff's Office

Kmart™

Kohl's®

Kroger Company® - Atlanta, GA Division

L.L. Bean Factory Store™

L.L. Bean Kids™

L.L. Bean™

La Crescenta (CA) Sheriff's Department

LaBonne's - Naugatuck, CT

Lake County (IN) Public Library System

Las Vegas (NV) Clark County Library District

Lawrence (KS) Public Library

Lazar Skate Play Palace

Lehigh Valley (PA) Zoo

Lemont (OH) Park District

Libertyville (IL) Parks and Recreation Department

Life Time Fitness®

LifeCenter Plus - Hudson, OH

Limited Brands, Inc.®

Linens-N-Things®

Lisle (IL) Park District

Little Flower Catholic School - Indianapolis, IN

Lofino Food Stores, Inc.

Logomotion Embroidery Company, Inc.™

Long's Drug Stores, Inc.™

Looney's Superskate

Los Alamos (NM) Medical Center

Loudoun County (VA) Public Library

Louisiana Children's Museum

Lowe's Home Improvement Warehouse™

M.N. Goldseins Co., Inc.

Macy's™ - Salem, Oregon Locations

Magic Springs & Crystal Falls™

Magnolia Regional Health Care Center - Corinth, MS

Maine Missing Children's Clearinghouse

Malco Theatres, Inc.

Mann Theatres - St Louis (MN) Park Cinema 6

Marana (AZ) Police Department

Maranthon Community Church

Marion (SC) County Health Department

Marion (SC) Police Department

Marketplace Foods

Marshall Community Center - Vancouver, WA

Marshall County (IN) Sheriff's Department

Marshall's®

Martins Super Markets

Mary Chiles Hospital - Mt. Sterling, KY

Mathis Brothers Furniture

MC Management Co. Inc.

Mease Countryside Hospital - Safety Harbor, FL

Mega Pick'n Save East

Menards

Mercy Outpatient Rehab Center - Roseville, CA

Merritt Athletic Clubs

Michael's Stores, Inc.®

Micheal Memorial - Gulfport, MS

Michigan Department of State Police

Michigan Hapkido Academy

Mid-America Management Corporation®

Middle Country Public Library - Centereach, NY

Mill Mountain Zoo

Mills Fleet Farm

Miskelly Furniture

Missing Child Center-Hawaii

Mississippi Attorney General's Office

Missouri State Highway Patrol - DDCC

Morris County (NJ) Park Police

Morris Furniture Ashley Homestore

MOSSystems - Clarendon, NY

Mountain Empire (VA) Community College

Mr. Treasures Xchange™

Mt. Clemens (MN) General Hospital Emergency Department

Mt. Pleasant (IA) Public Library

Mt. San Rafael Hospital - Trinidad, CO

Museum of Natural and Cultural History - Eugene, OR

Museum of Science and Industry, Chicago SM

Museum Place Mall

National Cowgirl Museum and Hall of Fame

National Institutes of Health

Native American Community Health Center - Phoenix, AZ

Natural Tunnel State Park

Navy Exchange Service Command SM

NC Transportation Museum

New Hampshire Attorney General's Office

New Jersey State Police

New Mexico Skate, Inc.

Nick's Pizza & Pub - Crystal Lake, IL

Nordstrom™

Norridge (IL) Park District's ECE

North American Cinemas, Inc.

North Carolina Aquarium at Ft. Fisher

North Carolina Aquarium at Pine Knoll Shores

North Carolina Aquarium on Roanoke Island

North Carolina Transportation Museum

North Clackamas (OR) Aquatic Park

Northbrook (IL) Park District

Northline (TX) Mall

Norton Simon Museum

Oak Forest (IL) Park District

Oak Lawn (IL) Park District™

Ocean City (NJ) Public Library

Ocean County (NJ) Library

Ocean Shores IGA

Ocean State Job Lot

Odenville (AL) Public Library

Office Depot®

Office Max®

Office Of Management and Budget of the Commonwealth of Puerto Rico

Old Country Buffet™

Old Navy®

Old Time Pottery, Inc.®

OLPD Pools

Omni Richmond (VA) Hotel

One World Community Health Center - Omaha, NE

Orange County (FL) Regional History Center

Oro Valley (AZ) Public Library

OSF St. Francis Medical Center - Peoria, IL

Oshman's Sporting Good Stores™

Pace, Inc.

Palmetto (SC) Health Richland - Columbia, SC

Park District of Forest Park (IL)

Park District of Highland Park® (IL)

Parker County (TX) Search and Rescue Team

Parrot Jungle Island™

Party City Corporation®

Party City Holding LLC™

Patchogue-Medford (NY) Public Library

Pathmark Supermarket™

Paul D. Camp Community College

Pekin (IL) Public Library

Pella (IA) Public Library

Pennsylvania House of Representatives

Peoria (IL) Park District

Pet Quarters of Maine

PETCO™

Petsmart®

Pheasant Run Resort

Philadelphia Museum of Art

Piggly Wiggly®

Pima Unified School District (AZ)

Pinheads

Pittsburgh (PA) Children's Museum

Play Café SM

Playland Amusement Park

Prevailing Word Christian Center - Plantation, FL

Prince George's (MD) Muslim Association

Project Safe Children®

Prospect Park (NY) Zoo

Provena Mercy Center Hospital - Aurora, IL

Public Buildings Authority of Puerto Rico

Publix®

Puerto Rico Electric Power Authority

Rapids (WI) Mall®

Ray Lewis & Company

RC Willey®

Real Estate Resources - Charleston, WV

Recreation Equipment Inc.®

Reliant Client Services

Retail Marketing Services™ - San Diego, CA

Reyna School for Boys

Rightmer, Inc.™

River Oaks (MO) Care Center

Riverhead Free Library - Riverhead, NY

Rockford (IL) Public Library

Rocky's Ace Hardware®

Rogers (NY) Memorial Library

Rollhaven Skate & Fun Center - Flint, MI

Rose Hill Townhouses, Inc.

Rowe's Supermarkets SM

RPCS, Inc.®

Saddleback College

Safeway, Inc.™

Saint Paul (MN) Public Library

Salvation Army - Western Territory

San Jose (CA) Public Library

Sav-A-Center™

Savannah (GA) Christian Church

Save On Foods™

Saved By The Cross Ministries - Mosinee, WI

Science Central - Fort Wayne, IN

Science Museum of Virginia

Scrapbook Studio™

Sears®

Shakopee (MN) Cub Foods

Shaw's Supermarkets, Inc™

Shawnee (KS) United Methodist Church

Shop-Rite - Edison, NJ

Sienna Crossing (TX) Elementary School

Singewald's ATA Black Belt Leadership Academy

Skateland Playdaze

Skatetown - Enid, OK

Smith, Inc.®

Soaring Eagle Casino & Resort

Sobeys West™

South River Compounding Pharmacy - Richmond, VA

SpecialFX Sports, Inc

Speed Art Museum - Louisville, KY

Sportman's Warehouse SM

Sports Authority®

St. Catherine School - Milwaukee, WI

St. Mary Medical Center - Walla Walla, WA

Stage Stores

Stanford University Bookstore

Star Market - Hyannis, MA

Stater Bros. Markets

Steve & Barry's University Sportswear SM

Sugar N Spice Child Care - Scranton, PA

Sunrise (NV) Public Library

Sunset Empire Parks and Rec® - Seaside, OR

Sunshine Foods

Superfresh®

Supervalu, Inc.

Sweetbay Supermarkets™ - Naples, FL

T & B Enterprise

T.J. Maxx®

Tama (IA) Public Library

Tampa (FL) Fire Rescue

Tanger Outlet Center™

Target®

Temple Christian School - West Carollton, OH

The Brentwood (TN) Library

The Crossing, A Christian Church

The Furniture Store®

The Houston (TX) Museum of Natural Science

The Kerley Group

The Ohio Historical Society

The Portillo Restaurant Group®

The Ritz Theatre Company, Inc.

The Smithtown (NY) Library

The Wackenhut Corporation

The Welk Resort Branson

Thomas Nelson Community College® - Hampton, VA

Tidewater (VA) Community College

Tidyman's, LLC SM

Tigard (OR) Public Library

Time In Franchises, LLC

Time In Interactive Play and Party Centers

Tippah County (MS) Sheriff's Office

Tishman Speyer ™

TJX®

Topeka and Shawnee (KS) County Public Library

Town & Country Skateworld

Toys "R" Us, Inc.™

Tuesday Morning, Inc.®

Tykes Town, Inc.

Tyler Motorsports™

U.S. Department of Defense

U.S. Department of Homeland Security

U.S. Department of Transportation

U.S. Federal Protective Service

U.S. General Services Administration

U.S. General Services Administration

U.S. Marshal Service

Ukrop's™

United Skates of America™

United Way of Sussex County™ (NJ)

University Christian Fellowship

University Recreation, Washington State University

Upper Nazareth (PA) Police Department

Uptown Technologies®

VaCap Federal Credit Union

Vallco Fashion Park SM

Value City®

Victoria Rapid Transit, Inc.®

Victory Child Care, Inc.

Village of Pinecrest/Pinecrest Gardens (FL)

Vineyard of the Canyon Church

Virgin Entertainment Group

Virginia Attorney General's Office

Virginia Beach (VA) Department of Public Health

Virginia Center Commons

Virginia Department of Motor Vehicles

Virginia Department of Rehabilitative Services

Virginia Department of Transportation

Virginia Zoological Society

Waldbaums

Walgreen®

Wal-Mart® Stores, Inc.

Warehouse Shoe Sale®

Warren General Hospital®

Warsaw (IN) Community Public Library

Washington State Division of Child Support

Watson's Laboratories, Inc.

Waukegan (IL) Park District

Wedding Tree Printing

West Charleston (NV) Library

West Chicago (IL) Park District

Wheelie Fun, Inc. - Accord, NY

Wheeling Park (IL) District

Whitney (NV) Library

Whole Foods Market®

Winnipeg (MB) Goldeyes Baseball Club

Winnipeg (MB) Public Library System

World Market™

Worsley's SM

Wow Family Fun Center™

Xanterra (CA) Parks & Resort®

YMCA®

Zanesville (OH) Surgery Center

APPENDIX 8:
UNIFORM CHILD CUSTODY JURISDICTION ACT

SECTION 1. PURPOSES OF ACT; CONSTRUCTION OF PROVISIONS.

(a) The general purposes of this Act are to:

(1) avoid jurisdictional competition and conflict with courts of other states in matters of child custody which have in the past resulted in the shifting of children from state to state with harmful effects on their well-being;

(2) promote cooperation with the courts of other states to the end that a custody decree is rendered in that state which can best decide the case in the interest of the child;

(3) assure that litigation concerning the custody of a child take place ordinarily in the state with which the child and his family have the closest connection and where significant evidence concerning his care, protection, training, and personal relationships is most readily available, and the courts of this state decline the exercise of jurisdiction when the child and his family have a closer connection with another state;

(4) discourage continuing controversies over child custody in the interest of greater stability of home environment and of secure family relationships for the child;

(5) deter abductions and other unilateral removals of children undertaken to obtain custody awards;

(6) avoid re-litigation of custody decisions of other states in this state insofar as feasible;

(7) facilitate the enforcement of custody decrees of other states;

(8) promote and expand the exchange of information and other forms of mutual assistance between the courts of this state and those of other states concerned with the same child; and

(9) make uniform the law of those states which enact it.

(b) this Act shall be construed to promote the general purposes stated in this section.

SECTION 2. DEFINITIONS. AS USED IN THIS ACT:

(1) "contestant" means a person, including a parent, who claims a right to custody or visitation rights with respect to a child;

(2) "custody determination" means a court decision and court orders and instructions providing for the custody of a child, including visitation rights; it does not include a decision relating to child support or any other monetary obligation of any person;

(3) "custody proceeding" includes proceedings in which a custody determination is one of several issues, such as an action for divorce or separation, and includes child neglect and dependency proceedings;

(4) "decree" or "custody decree" means a custody determination contained in a judicial decree or order made in a custody proceeding, and includes an initial decree and a modification decree;

(5) "home state" means the state in which the child immediately preceding the time involved lived with his parents, a parent, or a person acting as parent, for at least 6 consecutive months, and in the case of a child less than 6 months old the state in which the child lived from birth with any of the persons mentioned. Periods of temporary absence of any of the named persons are counted as part of the 6-month or other period;

(6) "initial decree" means the first custody decree concerning a particular child;

(7) "modification decree" means a custody decree which modifies or replaces a prior decree, whether made by the court which rendered the prior decree or by another court;

(8) "physical custody" means actual possession and control of a child;

(9) "person acting as parent" means a person, other than a parent, who has physical custody of a child and who has either been awarded custody by a court or claims a right to custody; and

(10) "state" means any state, territory, or possession of the United States, the Commonwealth of Puerto Rico, and the District of Columbia.

* * *

SECTION 7. INCONVENIENT FORUM.

(a) A court which has jurisdiction under this Act to make an initial or modification decree may decline to exercise its jurisdiction any time before making a decree if it finds that it is an inconvenient forum to make a custody determination under the circumstances of the case and that a court of another State is a more appropriate forum;

(b) A finding of inconvenient forum may be made upon the court's own motion or upon motion of a party or a guardian ad litem or other representative of the child;

(c) In determining if it is an inconvenient forum, the court shall consider if it is in the interest of the child that another state assume jurisdiction. For this purpose it may take into account the following factors, among others:

(1) if another state is or recently was the child's home state;

(2) if another state has a closer connection with the child and his family or with the child and one or more of the contestants;

(3) if substantial evidence concerning the child's present or future care, protection, training, and personal relationships is more readily available in another state;

(4) if the parties have agreed on another forum which is no less appropriate; and

(5) if the exercise of jurisdiction by a court of this State would contravene any of the purposes stated in section 1.

(d) Before determining whether to decline or retain jurisdiction the court may communicate with a court of another state and exchange information pertinent to the assumption of jurisdiction by either court with a view to assuring that jurisdiction will be exercised by the appropriate court and that a forum will be available to the parties.

(e) If the court finds that it is an inconvenient forum and that a court of another state is a more appropriate forum, it may dismiss the proceedings, or it may stay the proceedings upon condition that a custody proceeding be promptly commenced in another named state or upon any other conditions which may be just and proper; including the condition that a moving party stipulate his consent and submission to the jurisdiction of the other forum.

(f) The court may decline to exercise its jurisdiction under this Act if a custody determination is incidental to an action for divorce or another proceeding while retaining jurisdiction of the other forum.

(g) If it appears to the court that it is clearly an inappropriate forum it may require the party who commenced the proceedings to pay, in addition to the costs of the proceedings in this State, necessary travel and other expenses, including attorney's fees, incurred by other parties or their witnesses. Payment is to be made to the clerk of the court for remittance to the proper party.

(h) Upon dismissal or stay of proceedings under this section the court shall inform the court found to be the more appropriate forum of this fact, or if the court which would have jurisdiction in the other state is not certainly known, shall transmit the information to the court administrator or other appropriate official for forwarding to the appropriate party.

(i) Any communication received from another state informing this State of a finding of inconvenient forum because this State is the more appropriate forum shall be filed in the custody registry of the appropriate court. Upon assuming jurisdiction the court of this State shall inform the original court of this fact.

SECTION 8. JURISDICTION DECLINED BY REASON OF CONDUCT.

(a) If the petitioner for an initial decree has wrongfully taken the child from another state or has engaged in similar reprehensible conduct the court may decline to exercise jurisdiction if this is just and proper under the circumstances.

(b) Unless required in the interest of the child, the court shall not exercise its jurisdiction to modify a custody decree of another state if the petitioner, without consent of the person entitled to custody, has improperly removed the child from the physical custody of the person entitled to custody or has improperly retained the child after a visit or other temporary relinquishment of physical custody. If the petitioner has violated any other provision of a custody decree of another state the court may decline to exercise its jurisdiction if this is just and proper under the circumstances.

(c) In appropriate cases a court dismissing a petition under this section may charge the petitioner with necessary travel and other expenses, including attorney's fees, incurred by other parties or their witnesses.

SECTION 9. INFORMATION UNDER OATH TO BE SUBMITTED TO THE COURT.

(a) Every party in a custody proceeding in his first pleading or in an affidavit attached to that pleading shall give information under oath as to the child's present address, the places where the child has lived within the last 5 years, and the names and present addresses of the person with whom the child has lived during that period. In this pleading or affidavit every party shall further declare under oath whether:

(1) he has participated (as a party, witness, or in any other capacity) in any other litigation concerning the custody of the same child in this or any other state;

(2) he has information of any custody proceeding concerning the child pending in a court of this or any other state; and

(3) he knows of any person not a party to the proceedings who has physical custody of the child or claims to have custody or visitation with respect to the child.

(b) If the declaration as to any of the above items is in the affirmative the declarant shall give additional information under oath as to details of the information furnished and as to other matters pertinent to the court's jurisdiction and the disposition of the case.

(c) Each party has a continuing duty to inform the court of any custody proceeding concerning the child in this or any other state of which he obtained information during this proceeding.

SECTION 10. ADDITIONAL PARTIES.

If the court learns from information furnished by the parties pursuant to section 9 or from other sources that a person not a party to the custody proceeding has physical custody of the child or claims to have custody or visitation rights with respect to the child, it shall order that person to be joined as a party and to be duly notified of the pendency of the proceeding and of his joinder as a party. If the person joined as a party is outside this State he shall be served with process or otherwise notified in accordance with section 5.

SECTION 11. APPEARANCE OF PARTIES AND THE CHILD.

(a) The court may order any party to the proceeding who is in this State to appear personally before the court. If that party has physical custody of the child the court may order that he appear personally with the child.

(b) If a party to the proceeding whose presence is desired by the court is outside this State with or without the child the court may order that the notice given under section 5 include a statement directing that party to appear personally with or without the child declaring that failure to appear may result in a decision adverse to that party.

(c) If a party to the proceeding who is outside this State is directed to appear under subsection (b) or desires to appear personally before the court with or without the child, the court may require another party to pay to the clerk of the court travel and other necessary expenses of the party so appearing and of the child if this is just and proper under the circumstances.

SECTION 12. BINDING FORCE AND RES JUDICATA EFFECT OF CUSTODY DECREE.

A custody decree rendered by a court of this State which had jurisdiction under section 3 binds all parties who have been served in this State or notified in accordance with section 5 or who have submitted to the jurisdiction of the court, and who have been given an opportunity to be heard. As to these parties the custody decree is conclusive as to all issues of law and fact decided and as to the custody determination made unless and until that determination is modified pursuant to law, including the provisions of this Act.

SECTION 13. RECOGNITION OF OUT-OF-STATE CUSTODY DECREE.

The courts of this State shall recognize and enforce an initial or modification decree of a court of another state which had assumed jurisdiction under statutory provisions substantially in accordance with this Act or which was made under factual circumstances meeting the jurisdiction standards of the Act, so long as this decree has not been modified in accordance with jurisdictional standards substantially similar to those of this Act.

SECTION 14. MODIFICATION OF CUSTODY DECREE OF ANOTHER STATE.

(a) If a court of another state has made a custody decree, a court of this State shall not modify that decree unless (1) it appears to the court of this State that the court which rendered the decree does not now have jurisdiction under jurisdictional prerequisites substantially in accordance with this Act or has declined to assume jurisdiction to modify the decree and (2) the court of this State has jurisdiction.

(b) If a court of this State is authorized under subsection (a) and section 8 to modify a custody decree of another state it shall give due consideration to the transcript of the record and other documents of all previous proceedings submitted to it in accordance with section 22.

SECTION 15. FILING AND ENFORCEMENT OF CUSTODY DECREE OF ANOTHER STATE.

(a) A certified copy of a custody decree of another state may be filed in the office of the clerk of any [District Court, Family Court] of this State.

The clerk shall treat the decree in the same manner as a custody decree of the [District Court, Family Court] of this State. A custody decree so filed has the same effect and shall be enforced in like manner as a custody decree rendered by a court of this State.

(b) A person violating a custody decree of another state which makes it necessary to enforce the decree in this State may be required to pay necessary travel and other expenses, including attorneys' fees, incurred by the party entitled to the custody or his witnesses.

SECTION 16. REGISTRY OF OUT-OF-STATE CUSTODY DECREES AND PROCEEDINGS.

The clerk of each [District Court, Family Court] shall maintain a registry in which he shall enter the following:

(1) certified copies of custody decrees of other states received for filing;

(2) communications as to the pendency of custody proceedings in other states;

(3) communications concerning a finding of inconvenient forum by a court of another state; and

(4) other communications or documents concerning custody proceedings in another state which may affect the jurisdiction of a court of this State or the disposition to be made by it in a custody proceeding.

SECTION 17. CERTIFIED COPIES OF CUSTODY DECREE.

The Clerk of the [District Court, Family Court] of this State, at the request of the court of another state or at the request of any person who is affected by or has a legitimate interest in a custody decree, shall certify and forward a copy of the decree to that court or person.

SECTION 18. TAKING TESTIMONY IN ANOTHER STATE.

In addition to other procedural devices available to a party, any party to the proceeding or a guardian ad litem or other representative of the child may adduce testimony of witnesses, including parties and the child, by deposition or otherwise, in another state. The court on its own motion may direct that the testimony of a person be taken in another state and may prescribe the manner in which and the terms upon which the testimony shall be taken.

SECTION 19. HEARING AND STUDIES IN ANOTHER STATE; ORDERS TO APPEAL.

(a) A court of this State may request the appropriate court of another state to hold a hearing to adduce evidence, to order a party to produce or give evidence under other procedures of that state, or to have social studies made with respect to the custody of a child involved in proceedings pending in the court of this State; and to forward to the court of this State certified copies of the transcript of the record of the hearing, the evidence otherwise adduced, or any social studies prepared in compliance with the request. The cost of the services may be assessed against the parties or if necessary, ordered paid by the [County, State].

(b) A court of this State may request the appropriate court of another state to order a party to custody proceedings pending in the court of this State to appear in the proceedings, and if that party has physical custody of the child, to appear with the child. The request may state that travel and other necessary expenses of the party and of the child whose appearance is desired will be assessed against another party or will otherwise be paid.

SECTION 20. ASSISTANCE TO COURTS OF OTHER STATES.

(a) Upon request of the court of another state the courts of this State which are competent to hear custody matters may offer a person in this State to appear at a hearing to adduce evidence or to produce or give evidence under other procedures available in this State [or may order social studies to be made for use in a custody proceeding in another state]. A certified copy of the transcript of the record of the hearing or the evidence otherwise adduced [and any social studies prepared] shall be forwarded by the clerk of the court to the requesting court.

(b) A person within this State may voluntarily give his testimony or statement in this State for use in a custody proceeding outside this State.

(c) Upon request of the court of another state a competent court of this State may order a person in this State to appear alone or with the child in a custody proceeding in another state. The court may condition compliance with the request upon assurance by the other state that state travel and other necessary expenses will be advanced or reimbursed.

SECTION 21. PRESERVATION OF DOCUMENTS FOR USE IN OTHER STATES.

In any custody proceeding in this State the court shall preserve the pleadings, orders and decrees, any record that has been made of its hearing, social studies, and other pertinent documents until the child reaches [18, 21] years of age. Upon appropriate request of the court of another state the court shall forward to the other court certified copies of any or all of such documents.

SECTION 22. REQUEST FOR COURT RECORDS OF ANOTHER STATE.

If a custody decree has been rendered in another state concerning a child involved in a custody proceeding pending in a court of this State, the court of this State upon taking jurisdiction of the case shall request the court record and other documents mentioned in section 21.

SECTION 23. INTERNATIONAL APPLICATION.

The general policies of this Act extend to the international area. The provisions of this Act relating to the recognition and enforcement of custody decrees of other states apply to custody decrees and decrees involving legal institutions similar in nature to custody institutions rendered by appropriate authorities of other nations if reasonable notice and opportunity to be heard were given to all affected persons.

SECTION 24. PRIORITY.

Upon the request of a party to a custody proceeding which raises a question of existence or exercise of jurisdiction under this Act the case shall be given calendar priority and handled expeditiously.

SECTION 25. SEVERABILITY.

If any provisions of this Act or the application thereof to any person or circumstance is held invalid, its invalidity does not affect other provisions or applications of the Act which can be given effect without the invalid provision or application, and to this end the provisions of this Act are severable.

SECTION 26. SHORT TITLE.

This Act may be cited as the Uniform Child Custody Jurisdiction Act.

SECTION 27. REPEAL.

The following acts and parts of acts are repealed:

[State to provide]

SECTION 28. TIME OF TAKING EFFECT.

[State to provide]

APPENDIX 9:
PARENTAL KIDNAPPING PREVENTION ACT OF 1980

28 U.S.C. § 1738A. FULL FAITH AND CREDIT GIVEN TO CHILD CUSTODY DETERMINATIONS

(a) The appropriate authorities of every State shall enforce according to its terms, and shall not modify except as provided in subsection (f) of this section, any child custody determination made consistently with the provisions of this section by a court of another State.

(b) As used in this section, the term—

(1) "child" means a person under the age of eighteen;

(2) "contestant" means a person, including a parent, who claims a right to custody or visitation of a child;

(3) "custody determination" means a judgment, decree, or other order of a court providing for the custody or visitation of a child, and includes permanent and temporary orders, and initial orders and modifications;

(4) "home State" means the State in which, immediately preceding the time involved, the child lived with his parents, a parent, or a person acting as parent, for at least six consecutive months, and in the case of a child less than six months old, the State in which the child lived from birth with any of such persons. Periods of temporary absence of any of such persons are counted as part of the six-month or other period;

(5) "modification" and "modify" refer to a custody determination which modifies, replaces, supersedes, or otherwise is made subsequent to, a prior custody determination concerning the same child, whether made by the same court or not;

(6) "person acting as a parent" means a person, other than a parent, who has physical custody of a child and who has either been awarded custody by a court or claims a right to custody;

(7) "physical custody" means actual possession and control of a child; and

(8) "State" means a State of the United States, the District of Columbia, the Commonwealth of Puerto Rico, or a territory or possession of the United States.

(c) A child custody determination made by a court of a State is consistent with the provisions of this section only if—

(1) such court has jurisdiction under the law of such State; and

(2) one of the following conditions is met:

(A) such State (i) is the home State of the child on the date of the commencement of the proceeding, or (ii) had been the child's home State within six months before the date of the commencement of the proceeding and the child is absent from such State because of his removal or retention by a contestant or for other reasons, and a contestant continues to live in such State;

(B)(i) it appears that no other State would have jurisdiction under subparagraph (A), and (ii) it is in the best interest of the child that a court of such State assume jurisdiction because (I) the child and his parents, or the child and at least one contestant, have a significant connection with such State other than mere physical presence in such State and (II) there is available in such state substantial evidence concerning the child's present or future care, protection, training, and personal relationships;

(C) the child is physically present in such State and (i) the child has been abandoned, or (ii) it is necessary in an emergency to protect the child because he has been subjected to or threatened with mistreatment or abuse;

(D) (i) it appears that no other State would have jurisdiction under subparagraph (A), (B), (C), or (E), or another State has declined to exercise jurisdiction on the ground that the State whose jurisdiction is in issue is the more appropriate forum to determine the custody of the child, and (ii) it is in the best interest of the child that such court assume jurisdiction; or

(E) the court has continuing jurisdiction pursuant to subsection (d).

(d) The jurisdiction of a court of a State which has made a custody determination consistently with the provisions of this section continues as long as the requirement of subsection (c)(l) continues to be met and such State remains the residence of the child or of any contestant.

(e) Before a child custody determination is made, reasonable notice and opportunity to be heard shall be given to the contestants, any parent whose parental rights have not been previously terminated and any person who has physical custody of a child.

(f) A court of a State may modify a determination of the custody of the same child made by a court of another State, if—

(1) it has jurisdiction to make a child custody determination; and

(2) the court of the other State no longer has jurisdiction, or it has declined to exercise such jurisdiction to modify such determination.

(g) A court of a State shall not exercise jurisdiction in any proceeding for a custody determination commenced during the pendency of a proceeding in a court of another State where such court of that other State is exercising jurisdiction consistently with the provisions of this section to make a custody determination.

APPENDIX 10:
JURISDICTIONS THAT HAVE ENACTED THE UNIFORM CHILD-CUSTODY JURISDICTION AND ENFORCEMENT ACT (UCCJEA)

ALABAMA
ALASKA
ARIZONA
ARKANSAS
CALIFORNIA
COLORADO
CONNECTICUT
DELAWARE
DISTRICT OF COLUMBIA
FLORIDA
GEORGIA
HAWAII
IDAHO
ILLINOIS
IOWA
KANSAS
KENTUCKY
MAINE
MARYLAND
MICHIGAN
MINNESOTA

MISSISSIPPI
MONTANA
NEBRASKA
NEVADA
NEW JERSEY
NEW MEXICO
NEW YORK
NORTH CAROLINA
NORTH DAKOTA
OHIO
OKLAHOMA
OREGON
PENNSYLVANIA
RHODE ISLAND
TENNESSEE
TEXAS
UTAH
VIRGINIA
WASHINGTON
WEST VIRGINIA

SOURCE: U.S. Department of Justice.

APPENDIX 11:
HAGUE CONVENTION ON THE CIVIL ASPECTS OF INTERNATIONAL CHILD ABDUCTION

The States signatory to the present Convention, firmly convinced that the interests of children are of paramount importance in matters relating to their custody, desiring to protect children internationally from the harmful effects of their wrongful removal or retention and to establish procedures to ensure their prompt return to the State of their habitual residence, as well as to secure protection for rights of access, have resolved to conclude a Convention to this effect, and have agreed upon the following provisions—

CHAPTER I— SCOPE OF THE CONVENTION

ARTICLE 1

The objects of the present Convention are—

(a) to secure the prompt return of children wrongfully removed to or retained in any Contracting State; and

(b) to ensure that rights of custody and of access under the law of one Contracting State are effectively respected in other Contracting States.

ARTICLE 2

Contracting States shall take all appropriate measures to secure within their territories the implementation of the objects of the Convention. For this purpose they shall use the most expeditious procedures available.

ARTICLE 3

The removal or the retention of a child is to be considered wrongful where—

(a) it is in breach of rights of custody attributed to a person, an institution or any other body, either jointly or alone, under the law of the State in which the child was habitually resident immediately before the removal or retention; and

(b) at the time of removal or retention those rights were actually exercised, either jointly or alone, or would have been so exercised but for the removal or retention. The rights of custody mentioned in sub-paragraph a above, may arise in particular by operation of law or by reason of a judicial or administrative decision, or by reason of an agreement having legal effect under the law of that State.

ARTICLE 4

The Convention shall apply to any child who was habitually resident in a Contracting State immediately before any breach of custody or access rights. The Convention shall cease to apply when the child attains the age of 16 years.

ARTICLE 5

For the purposes of this Convention—

(a) 'rights of custody' shall include rights relating to the care of the person of the child and, in particular, the right to determine the child's place of residence;

(b) 'rights of access' shall include the right to take a child for a limited period of time to a place other than the child's habitual residence.

CHAPTER II— CENTRAL AUTHORITIES

ARTICLE 6

A Contracting State shall designate a Central Authority to discharge the duties which are imposed by the Convention upon such authorities. Federal States, States with more than one system of law or States having autonomous territorial organizations shall be free to appoint more than one Central Authority and to specify the territorial extent of their powers. Where a State has appointed more than one Central Authority, it shall designate the Central Authority to which applications may be addressed for transmission to the appropriate Central Authority within that State.

ARTICLE 7

Central Authorities shall co-operate with each other and promote co-operation amongst the competent authorities in their respective States to secure the prompt return of children and to achieve the other objects of this Convention. In particular, either directly or through any intermediary, they shall take all appropriate measures—

(a) to discover the whereabouts of a child who has been wrongfully removed or retained;

(b) to prevent further harm to the child or prejudice to interested parties by taking or causing to be taken provisional measures;

(c) to secure the voluntary return of the child or to bring about an amicable resolution of the issues;

(d) to exchange, where desirable, information relating to the social background of the child;

(e) to provide information of a general character as to the law of their State in connection with the application of the Convention;

(f) to initiate or facilitate the institution of judicial or administrative proceedings with a view to obtaining the return of the child and, in a proper case, to make arrangements for organizing or securing the effective exercise of rights of access;

(g) where the circumstances so require, to provide or facilitate the provision of legal aid and advice, including the participation of legal counsel and advisers;

(h) to provide such administrative arrangements as may be necessary and appropriate to secure the safe return of the child;

(i) to keep each other informed with respect to the operation of this Convention and, as far as possible, to eliminate any obstacles to its application.

CHAPTER III— RETURN OF CHILDREN

ARTICLE 8

Any person, institution or other body claiming that a child has been removed or retained in breach of custody rights may apply either to the Central Authority of the child's habitual residence or to the Central Authority of any other Contracting State for assistance in securing the return of the child.

The application shall contain—

(a) information concerning the identity of the applicant, of the child and of the person alleged to have removed or retained the child;

(b) where available, the date of birth of the child;

(c) the grounds on which the applicant's claim for return of the child is based;

(d) all available information relating to the whereabouts of the child and the identity of the person with whom the child is presumed to be.

The application may be accompanied or supplemented by—

(e) an authenticated copy of any relevant decision or agreement;

(f) a certificate or an affidavit emanating from a Central Authority, or other competent authority of the State of the child's habitual residence, or from a qualified person, concerning the relevant law of that State;

(g) any other relevant document.

ARTICLE 9

If the Central Authority which receives an application referred to in Article 8 has reason to believe that the child is in another Contracting State, it shall directly and without delay transmit the application to the Central Authority of that Contracting State and inform the requesting Central Authority, or the applicant, as the case may be.

ARTICLE 10

The Central Authority of the State where the child is shall take or cause to be taken all appropriate measures in order to obtain the voluntary return of the child.

ARTICLE 11

The judicial or administrative authorities of Contracting States shall act expeditiously in proceedings for the return of children.

If the judicial or administrative authority concerned has not reached a decision within six weeks from the date of commencement of the proceedings, the applicant or the Central Authority of the requested State, on its own initiative or if asked by the Central Authority of the requesting State, shall have the right to request a statement of the reasons for the delay. If a reply is received by the Central Authority of the requested State, that Authority shall transmit the reply to the Central Authority of the requesting State, or to the applicant, as the case may be.

ARTICLE 12

Where a child has been wrongfully removed or retained in terms of Article 3 and, at the date of the commencement of the proceedings before the judicial or administrative authority of the Contracting State where the child is, a period of less than one year has elapsed from the date of the wrongful removal or retention, the authority concerned shall order the return of the child forthwith.

The judicial or administrative authority, even where the proceedings have been commenced after the expiration of the period of one year referred to in the preceding paragraph, shall also order the return of the child, unless it is demonstrated that the child is now settled in its new environment.

Where the judicial or administrative authority in the requested State has reason to believe that the child has been taken to another State, it may stay the proceedings or dismiss the application for the return of the child.

ARTICLE 13

Notwithstanding the provisions of the preceding Article, the judicial or administrative authority of the requested State is not bound to order the return of the child if the person, institution or other body which opposes its return establishes that—

(a) the person, institution or other body having the care of the person of the child was not actually exercising the custody rights at the time of removal or retention, or had consented to or subsequently acquiesced in the removal of retention; or

(b) there is a grave risk that his or her return would expose the child to physical or psychological harm or otherwise place the child in an intolerable situation.

The judicial or administrative authority may also refuse to order the return of the child if it finds that the child objects to being returned and has attained an age and degree of maturity at which it is appropriate to take account of its views.

In considering the circumstances referred to in this Article, the judicial and administrative authorities shall take into account the information relating to the social background of the child provided by the Central Authority or other competent authority of the child's habitual residence.

ARTICLE 14

In ascertaining whether there has been a wrongful removal of retention within the meaning of Article 3, the judicial or administrative authorities of the requested State may take notice directly of the law of, and of judicial or administrative decisions, formally recognized or not in the State of the habitual residence of the child, without recourse to the specific procedures for the proof of that law or for the recognition of foreign decisions which would otherwise be applicable.

ARTICLE 15

The judicial or administrative authorities of a Contracting State may, prior to the making of an order for the return of the child, request that the applicant obtain from the authorities of the State of the habitual residence of the child a decision or other determination that the removal or retention was wrongful within the meaning of Article 3 of the Convention, where such a decision or determination may be obtained in that State. The Central Authorities of the Contracting States shall so far as practicable assist applicants to obtain such a decision or determination.

ARTICLE 16

After receiving notice of a wrongful removal or retention of a child in the sense of Article 3, the judicial or administrative authorities of the Contracting State to which the child has been removed or in which it has been retained shall not decide on the merits of rights of custody until it has been determined that the child is not to be returned under this Convention or unless an application under the Convention is not lodged within a reasonable time following receipt of the notice.

ARTICLE 17

The sole fact that a decision relating to custody has been given in or is entitled to recognition in the requested State shall not be a ground for refusing to return a child under this Convention, but the judicial or administrative authorities of the requested State may take account of the reasons for that decision in applying this Convention.

ARTICLE 18

The provisions of this Chapter do not limit the power of a judicial or administrative authority to order the return of the child at any time.

ARTICLE 19

A decision under this Convention concerning the return of the child shall not be taken to be determination on the merits of any custody issue.

ARTICLE 20

The return of the child under the provision of Article 12 may be refused if this would not be permitted by the fundamental principles of the requested State relating to the protection of human rights and fundamental freedoms.

CHAPTER IV— RIGHTS OF ACCESS

ARTICLE 21

An application to make arrangements for organizing or securing the effective exercise of rights of access may be presented to the Central Authorities of the Contracting States in the same way as an application for the return of a child.

The Central Authorities are bound by the obligations of co-operation which are set forth in Article 7 to promote the peaceful enjoyment of access rights and the fulfillment of any conditions to which the exercise of such rights may be subject. The Central Authorities shall take steps to remove, as far as possible, all obstacles to the exercise of such rights. The Central Authorities, either directly or through intermediaries, may initiate or assist in the institution of proceedings with a view to organizing or protecting these rights and securing respect for the conditions to which the exercise of these rights may be subject.

CHAPTER V— GENERAL PROVISIONS

ARTICLE 22

No security, bond or deposit, however described, shall be required to guarantee the payment of costs and expenses in the judicial or administrative proceedings falling within the scope of this Convention.

ARTICLE 23

No legalization or similar formality may be required in the context of this Convention.

ARTICLE 24

Any application, communication or other document sent to the Central Authority of the requested State shall be in the original language, and shall be accompanied by a translation into the official language or one of the official languages of the requested State or, where that is not feasible, a translation into French or English.

However, a Contracting State may, by making a reservation in accordance with Article 42, object to the use of either French or English, but not both, in any application, communication or other document sent to its Central Authority.

ARTICLE 25

Nationals of the Contracting States and persons who are habitually resident within those States shall be entitled in matters concerned with the application of this Convention to legal aid and advice in any other Contracting State on the same conditions as if they themselves were nationals of and habitually resident in that State.

ARTICLE 26

Each Central Authority shall bear its own costs in applying this Convention. Central Authorities and other public services of Contracting States shall not impose any charges in relation to applications submitted under this Convention. In particular, they may not require any payment from the applicant towards the costs and expenses of the proceedings or, where applicable, those arising from the participation of legal counsel or advisers.

However, they may require the payment of the expenses incurred or to be incurred in implementing the return of the child.

However, a Contracting State may, by making a reservation in accordance with Article 42, declare that it shall not be bound to assume any costs referred to in the preceding paragraph resulting from the participation of legal counsel or advisers or from court proceedings, except insofar as those costs may be covered by its system of legal aid and advice.

Upon ordering the return of a child or issuing an order concerning rights of access under this Convention, the judicial or administrative authorities may, where appropriate, direct the person who removed or retained the child, or who prevented the exercise of rights of access, to pay necessary expenses incurred by or on behalf of the applicant, including travel expenses, any costs incurred or payments made for locating the child, the costs of legal representation of the applicant, and those of returning the child.

ARTICLE 27

When it is manifest that the requirements of this Convention are not fulfilled or that the application is otherwise not well founded, a Central Authority is not bound to accept the application. In that case, the Central Authority shall forthwith inform the applicant or the Central Authority through which the application was submitted, as the case may be, of its reasons.

ARTICLE 28

A Central Authority may require that the application be accompanied by a written authorization empowering it to act on behalf of the applicant, or to designate a representative so to act.

ARTICLE 29

This Convention shall not preclude any person, institution or body who claims that there has been a breach of custody or access rights within the meaning of Article 3 or 21 from applying directly to the judicial or administrative authorities of a Contracting State, whether or not under the provisions of this Convention.

ARTICLE 30

Any application submitted to the Central Authorities or directly to the judicial or administrative authorities of a Contracting State in accordance with the terms of this Convention, together with documents and any other information appended thereto or provided by a Central Authority, shall be admissible in the courts or administrative authorities of the Contracting States.

ARTICLE 31

In relation to a State which in matters of custody of children has two or more systems of law applicable in different territorial units—

(a) any reference to habitual residence in that State shall be construed as referring to habitual residence in a territorial unit of that State;

(b) any reference to the law of the State of habitual residence shall be construed as referring to the law of the territorial unit in that State where the child habitually resides.

ARTICLE 32

In relation to a State which in matters of custody of children has two or more systems of law applicable to different categories of persons, any reference to the law of that State shall be construed as referring to the legal system specified by the law of that State.

ARTICLE 33

A State within which different territorial units have their own rules of law in respect of custody of children shall not be bound to apply this Convention where a State with a unified system of law would not be bound to do so.

ARTICLE 34

This Convention shall take priority in matters within its scope over the Convention of 5 October 1961 concerning the powers of authorities and the law applicable in respect of the protection of minors, as between Parties to both Conventions. Otherwise the present Convention shall not restrict the application of an international instrument in force between the State of origin and the State addressed or other law of the State addressed for the purposes of obtaining the return of a child who has been wrongfully removed or retained or of organizing access rights.

ARTICLE 35

This Convention shall apply as between Contracting States only to wrongful removals or retentions occurring after its entry into force in those States.

Where a declaration has been made under Article 39 or 40, the reference in the preceding paragraph to a Contracting State shall be taken to refer to the territorial unit or units in relation to which this Convention applies.

ARTICLE 36

Nothing in this Convention shall prevent two or more Contracting State, in order to limit the restrictions to which the return of the child may be subject, from agreeing among themselves to derogate from any provision of this Convention which may imply such a restriction.

CHAPTER VI— FINAL CLAUSES

ARTICLE 37

The Convention shall be open for signature by the States which were Members of the Hague Conference on Private International Law at the time of its Fourteenth Session. It shall be ratified, accepted or approved and the instruments of ratification, acceptance or approval shall be deposited with the Ministry of Foreign Affairs of the Kingdom of the Netherlands.

ARTICLE 38

Any other State may accede to the Convention. The instrument of accession shall be deposited with the Ministry of Foreign Affairs of the Kingdom of the Netherlands.

The Convention shall enter into force for a State acceding to it on the first day of the third calendar month after the deposit of its instrument of accession. The accession will have effect only as regards the relations between the acceding State and such Contracting States as will have declared their acceptance of the accession. Such a declaration will also have to be made by any Member State ratifying, accepting or approving the Convention after an accession. Such declaration shall be deposited at the Ministry of Foreign Affairs of the Kingdom of the Netherlands; this Ministry shall forward, through diplomatic channels, a certified copy to each of the Contracting States.

The Convention will enter into force as between the acceding State and the State that has declared its acceptance of the accession on the first day of the third calendar month after the deposit of the declaration of acceptance.

ARTICLE 39

Any State may, at the time of signature, ratification, acceptance, approval or accession, declare that the Convention shall extend to all the territories for the international relations of which it is responsible, or to one or more of them. Such a declaration shall take effect at the time the Convention enters into force for that State. Such declaration, as well as any subsequent extension, shall be notified to the Ministry of Foreign Affairs of the Kingdom of the Netherlands.

ARTICLE 40

If a Contracting State has two or more territorial units in which different systems of law are applicable in relation to matters dealt with in this Convention, it may at the time of signature, ratification, acceptance, approval or accession declare that this Convention shall extend to all its territorial units or only to one or more of them and may modify this declaration by submitting another declaration at any time. Any such declaration shall be notified to the Ministry of Foreign Affairs of the Kingdom of the Netherlands and shall state expressly the territorial units to which the Convention applies.

ARTICLE 41

Where a Contracting State has a system of government under which executive, judicial and legislative powers are distributed between central and other authorities within that State, its signature or ratification, acceptance or approval of, or accession to this Convention, or its making of any declaration in terms of Article 40 shall carry no implication as to the internal distribution of powers within that State.

ARTICLE 42

Any State may, not later than the time of ratification, acceptance, approval or accession, or at the time of making a declaration in terms of Article 39 or 40, make one or both of the reservations provided for in Article 24 and Article 26, third paragraph. No other reservations shall be permitted. Any State may at any time withdraw a reservation it has made. The withdraw shall be notified to the Ministry of Foreign Affairs of the Kingdom of the Netherlands. The reservation shall cease to have effect on the first day of the third calendar month after the notification referred to in the preceding paragraph.

ARTICLE 43

The Convention shall enter into force on the first day of the third calendar month after the deposit of the third instrument of ratification, acceptance, approval or accession referred to in Articles 37 and 38. Thereafter the Convention shall enter into force—

(1) for each State ratifying, accepting, approving or acceding to it subsequently, on the first day of the third calendar month after the deposit of its instrument of ratification, acceptance, approval or accession;

(2) for any territory or territorial unit to which the Convention has been extended in conformity with Article 39 or 40, on the first day of the third calendar month after the notification referred to in that Article.

ARTICLE 44

The Convention shall remain in force for five years form the date of its entry into force in accordance with the first paragraph of Article 43 even for States which subsequently have ratified, accepted, approved it or acceded to it. If there has been no denunciation, it shall be renewed tacitly every five years. Any denunciation shall be notified to the Ministry of Foreign Affairs of the Kingdom of the Netherlands at least six months before the expiry of the five year period. It may be limited to certain of the territories or territorial units to which the Convention applies.

The denunciation shall have effect only as regards the State which has notified it. The Convention shall remain in force for the other Contracting States.

ARTICLE 45

The Ministry of Foreign Affairs of the Kingdom of the Netherlands shall notify the States Members of the Conference, and the States which have acceded in accordance with Article 38, of the following—

(1) the signatures and ratifications, acceptances and approvals referred to in Article 37;

(2) the accession referred to in Article 38;

(3) the date on which the Convention enters into force in accordance with Article 43;

(4) the extensions referred to in Article 39;

(5) the declarations referred to in Articles 38 and 40;

(6) the reservations referred to in Article 24 and Article 26, third paragraph, and the withdrawals referred to in Article 42;

(7) the denunciation referred to in Article 44.

In witness whereof the undersigned, being duly authorized thereto, have signed this Convention.

Done at The Hague, on the 25th day of October, 1980, in the English and French languages, both texts being equally authentic, in a single copy which shall be deposited in the archives of the Government of the Kingdom of the Netherlands, and of which a certified copy shall be sent, through diplomatic channels, to each of the States Members of the Hague Conference on Private International Law at the date of its Fourteenth Session.

APPENDIX 12:
PARTIES TO THE HAGUE CONVENTION

COUNTRY	ENTRY DATE
ARGENTINA	June 1, 1991
AUSTRALIA	July 1, 1988
AUSTRIA	October 1,1988
BAHAMAS	January 1,1994
BELGIUM	May 1,1999
BELIZE	November 1, 1989
BERMUDA	March 1, 1999
BOSNIA AND HERZEGOVINA	December 1, 1991
BRAZIL	December 1, 2003
BULGARIA	January 1, 2005
BURKINA FASO	November 1, 1992
CANADA	July 1, 1988
CAYMAN ISLANDS	August 1, 1998
CHILE	July 1, 1994
CHINA	(Hong Kong Special Admin. Region- September 1, 1997); (Macau - March 1, 1999)
COLOMBIA	June 1, 1996
CROATIA	December 1, 1991
CZECH REPUBLIC	March 1, 1998
CYPRUS	March 1, 1995
DENMARK	July 1, 1991
ECUADOR	April 1, 1992
FINLAND	August 1, 1994
FRANCE	July 1, 1988

COUNTRY	ENTRY DATE
GERMANY	December 1, 1990
GREECE	June 1, 1993
HONDURAS	June 1, 1994
HUNGARY	Jul 1, 1988
ICELAND	December 1, 1996
IRELAND	October 1, 1991
ISLE OF MAN	September 1, 1991
ISRAEL	December 1, 1991
ITALY	May 1, 1995
LUXEMBOURG	July 1, 1988
MACEDONIA, FORMER YUGOSLAV REPUBLIC OF	December 1, 1991
MALTA	February 1, 2003
MAURITIUS	October 1, 1993
MEXICO	October 1, 1991
MONACO	June 1, 1993
MONTSERRAT	March 1, 1999
NETHERLANDS	September 1, 1990
NEW ZEALAND	October 1, 1991
NORWAY	April 1, 1989
PANAMA	June 1, 1994
POLAND	November 1, 1992
PORTUGAL	July 1, 1988
ROMANIA	June 1, 1993
SLOVAK REPUBLIC	February 1, 2001
SLOVENIA	April 1, 1995
SOUTH AFRICA	November 1, 1997
SPAIN	July 1, 1988
ST. KITTS AND NEVIS	June 1, 1995
SWEDEN	June 1, 1989
SWITZERLAND	July 1, 1988
TURKEY	August 1, 2000
URUGUAY	September 1, 2004
VENEZUELA	January 1, 1997

COUNTRY	ENTRY DATE
YUGOSLAVIA, FEDERAL REPUBLIC OF	December 1, 1991
ZIMBABWE	August 1, 1995

SOURCE: U.S. Department of State

APPENDIX 13:
DIRECTORY OF CENTRAL AUTHORITIES

MEMBER COUNTRY	CENTRAL AUTHORITY	WEBSITE
ARGENTINA	Ministry of Foreign Affairs	http://www.menores.gov.ar/
AUSTRALIA	Attorney General's Department	http://www.ag.gov.au/
AUSTRIA	Ministry of Justice	http://www.bmj.gv.at/
BAHAMAS	Ministry of Foreign Affairs	www.mfabahamas.org/
BELARUS	Ministry of Justice	http://ncpi.gov.by/minjust/
BELGIUM	Ministry of Justice	http://www.just.fgov.be/
BELIZE	Ministry of Human Development, Women, and Civil Society	http://www.belize.gov.bz/
BRAZIL	Ministry of Justice	http://www.mj.gov.br/
CANADA	Department of Justice	http://www.justice.gouv.qc.ca/
CHILE	Ministry of Justice	http://www.cajmetro.cl/
DENMARK	Ministry of Justice	http://www.boernebortfoerelse.dk/
FINLAND	Ministry of Justice	http://www.om.fi/20726.htm
FRANCE	Ministry of Justice	http://www.enlevement-parental.justice.gouv.fr/
GERMANY	Ministry of Justice	http://www.auswaertiges-amt.de/www/en/laenderinfos/konsulat/kindesentziehung.html
GREECE	Ministry of Justice	http://www.ministryofjustice.gr/
HUNGARY	Ministry of Justice	http://www.im.hu/
IRELAND	Department of Justice	http://www.justice.ie/

MEMBER COUNTRY	CENTRAL AUTHORITY	WEBSITE
ISRAEL	Ministry of Justice	http://www.justice.gov.il/
ITALY	Ministry of Justice	http://www.giustizia.it/
MEXICO	Ministry of Foreign Relations	http://www.sre.gob.mx/
NETHERLANDS	Ministry of Justice	http://www.minjus.nl/
NEW ZEALAND	Ministry of Justice	http://www.justice.govt.nz/
NORWAY	Ministry of Justice	http://odin.dep.no/jd/english/bn.html
POLAND	Ministry of Justice	http://www.ms.gov.pl/
PORTUGAL	Ministry of Foreign Affairs	http://www.mj.gov.pt/
SOUTH AFRICA	Justice Department	http://www.doj.gov.za/
SPAIN	Ministry of Justice	http://www.justicia.es/
SWEDEN	Ministry of Justice	http://www.sweden.gov.se/
SWITZERLAND	Ministry of Justice	http://www.ejpd.admin.ch/ejpd/de/home.html
TURKEY	Ministry of Justice	http://www.adalet.gov.tr/
UNITED KINGDOM (ENGLAND)	Department of Constitutional Affairs	http://www.dca.gov.uk/
UNITED KINGDOM (WALES)	Official Solicitor and Public Trustee	http://www.offsol.demon.co.uk/
UNITED KINGDOM (NORTHERN IRELAND)	Northern Ireland Office	http://www.nio.gov.uk/
UNITED KINGDOM (SCOTLAND)	Justice Department	http://www.scotland.gov.uk/
UNITED STATES OF AMERICA	Department of State	http://www.travel.state.gov/

APPENDIX 14:
ONLINE ACRONYMS

ACRONYM	MEANING
121	one to one
AFAIK	as far as I know
AFK	away from keyboard
AKA	also known as
ARE	acronym-rich environment
ASAP	as soon as possible
A/S/L	age, sex, location
B4	before
B4N	bye for now
BAK	back at the keyboard
BBIAB	be back in a bit
BBL	be back later
BBML	be back much later
BBN	bye bye now
BBS	be back soon
BEG	big evil grin
BF	boyfriend
BFN	bye for now
BG	big grin
BL	belly laughing
BRB	be right back
BTA	but then again
BTW	by the way
BWL	bursting with laughter
BWTHDIK	but what the heck do I know

ACRONYM	MEANING
C&G	chuckle & grin
CID	crying in disgrace
CNP	continued (in my) next post
CP	chat post
CRBT	crying real big tears
CSG	chuckle, snicker, grin
CU	see you
CUL or CUL8ER	see you later
CUZ	because
CYO	see you online
DIKU	do I know you?
DL	dead link
DLTBBB	don't let the bed bugs bite
DQMOT	don't quote me on this
EG	evil grin
EMFBI	excuse me for butting in
EOM	end of message
EOT	end of thread
F2F	face to face
FAQ	frequently asked question(s)
FC	fingers crossed
FISH	first in, still here
FMTYEWTK	far more than you ever wanted to know
FOMCL	falling off my chair laughing
FTBOMH	from the bottom of my heart
FUD	fear, uncertainty, and doubt
FWIW	for what it's worth
FYI	for your information
GA	go ahead
GAL	get a life
GD&R	grinning, ducking, & running
GF	girlfriend
GFN	gone for now
GIWIST	gee, I wish I'd said that

ACRONYM	MEANING
GMBO	giggling my butt off
GMTA	great minds think alike
GOL	giggling out loud
GTRM	going to read mail
GTSY	glad to see you
H&K	hug and kiss
HAGN	have a good night
HHIS	hanging head in shame
HTH	hope this helps
IAC	in any case
IAE	in any event
IANAL	I am not a lawyer (but)
IC	I see
IDK	I don't know
IHA	I hate acronyms
IIRC	if I remember correctly
ILU	I love you
IM	instant message
IMHO	in my humble opinion
IMing	chatting with someone online
IMNSHO	in my not so humble opinion
IMO	in my opinion
IOW	in other words
IPN	I'm posting naked
IRL	in real life
IWALU	I will always love you
IYSWIM	if you see what I mean
JBOD	just a bunch of disks
JIC	just in case
JK	just kidding
JMO	just my opinion
JTLYK	just to let you know
JW	just wondering
K	okay

ACRONYM	MEANING
KIT	keep in touch
KOC	kiss on cheek
KOL	kiss on lips
KWIM	know what I mean?
L2M	listening to music
L8R	later
LD	later, dude
LDR	long distance relationship
LHM	lord help me
LHU	lord help us
LLTA	lots and lots of thunderous applause
LMIRL	let's meet in real life
LMSO	laughing my socks off
LOL	laughing out loud
LRF	little rubber feet
LSHMBB	laughing so hard my belly is bouncing
LSHMBH	laughing so hard my belly hurts
LSHTTARDML	laughing so hard the tears are running down my leg
LTM	laugh to myself
LTNS	long time, no see
LTR	long term relationship
LTS	laughing to self
LULAB	love you like a brother
LULAS	love you like a sister
LUWAMH	love you with all my heart
LY	love you
M/F	male or female
MOSS	member of same sex
MOTOS	member of the opposite sex
MSG	message
MTF	more to follow
MUSM	miss you so much
NADT	not a darn thing
NIFOC	naked in front of computer

ACRONYM	MEANING
NP	nosy parents
N/P	no problem
NRN	no reply necessary
OIC	oh I see
OL	old lady
OLL	online love
OM	old man
OMG	oh my god
OTF	off the floor
OTOH	on the other hand
OTTOMH	off the top of my head
P2P	peer to peer
P911	my parents are coming!
PA	parent alert
PAL	parents are listening
PANB	parents are nearby
PANS	pretty awesome new stuff
PDA	public display of affection
PDS	please don't shoot
PLZ	please
PM	private message
PMFJIB	pardon me for jumping in but....
PMP	peed my pants
POAHF	put on a happy face
POS	parent over shoulder
POTS	plain old telephone service
PU	that stinks
QSL	reply
QSO	conversation
QT	cutie
RL	real life
ROL	raffing out loud
ROTFL	rolling on the floor laughing
RPG	role playing games

ACRONYM	MEANING
RSN	real soon now
RYO	roll your own
S4L	spam for life
SETE	smiling ear to ear
SF	surfer friendly
SHCOON	shoot hot coffee out of nose
SHID	slaps head in disgust
SNERT	snot nosed egotistical rude teenager
SO	significant other
SOMY	sick of me yet?
SOT	short of time
SOTMG	short of time, must go
STW	search the web
SUP or WU	what's up
SWAK	sealed with a kiss
SWL	screaming with laughter
SYS	see you soon
TA	thanks again
TAFN	that's all for now
TAW	teachers are watching
TCOB	taking care of business
TCOY	take care of yourself
TFH	thread from hell
TGIF	thank God it's Friday
THX	thanks
TIA	thanks in advance
TILII	tell it like it is
TLK2UL8R	talk to you later
TMI	too much information
TNT	'till next time
TOPCA	'til our paths cross again
TOY	thinking of you
TPTB	the powers that be
TTFN	ta ta for now

ACRONYM	MEANING
TTT	thought that too
TTYL	talk to you later
TU	thank you
UW	you're welcome
VBG	very big grin
WB	welcome back
WDALYIC	who died and left you in charge?
W/E	whatever
WFM	works for me
WIBNI	wouldn't it be nice if
WTG	way to go
WTGP	want to go private?
WTH	what/who the heck
WUF	where are you from?
WYSIWYG	what you see is what you get
YBS	you'll be sorry
YG	young gentleman
YL	young lady
YM	young man

APPENDIX 15:
THE CHILDREN'S ONLINE PRIVACY PROTECTION ACT (COPPA)

SEC. 1301. SHORT TITLE.

This title may be cited as the "Children's Online Privacy Protection Act of 1998".

SEC. 1302. DEFINITIONS.

In this title:

(1) CHILD.—The term "child" means an individual under the age of 13.

(2) OPERATOR.—The term "operator"—

(A) means any person who operates a website located on the Internet or an online service and who collects or maintains personal information from or about the users of or visitors to such website or online service, or on whose behalf such information is collected or maintained, where such website or online service is operated for commercial purposes, including any person offering products or services for sale through that website or online service, involving commerce—

(i) among the several States or with 1 or more foreign nations;

(ii) in any territory of the United States or in the District of Columbia, or between any such territory and—

(I) another such territory; or

(II) any State or foreign nation; or

(iii) between the District of Columbia and any State, territory, or foreign nation; but

(B) does not include any nonprofit entity that would otherwise be exempt from coverage under section 5 of the Federal Trade Commission Act (15 U.S.C. § 45).

(3) COMMISSION.—The term "Commission" means the Federal Trade Commission.

(4) DISCLOSURE.—The term "disclosure" means, with respect to personal information—

(A) the release of personal information collected from a child in identifiable form by an operator for any purpose, except where such information is provided to a person other than the operator who provides support for the internal operations of the website and does not disclose or use that information for any other purpose; and

(B) making personal information collected from a child by a website or online service directed to children or with actual knowledge that such information was collected from a child, publicly available in identifiable form, by any means including by a public posting, through the Internet, or through—

(i) a home page of a website;

(ii) a pen pal service;

(iii) an electronic mail service;

(iv) a message board; or

(v) a chat room.

(5) FEDERAL AGENCY.—The term "Federal agency" means an agency, as that term is defined in section 551(1) of title 5, United States Code.

(6) INTERNET.—The term "Internet" means collectively the myriad of computer and telecommunications facilities, including equipment and operating software, which comprise the interconnected world-wide network of networks that employ the Transmission Control Protocol/ Internet Protocol, or any predecessor or successor protocols to such protocol, to communicate information of all kinds by wire or radio.

(7) PARENT.—The term "parent" includes a legal guardian.

(8) PERSONAL INFORMATION.—The term "personal information" means individually identifiable information about an individual collected online, including—

(A) a first and last name;

(B) a home or other physical address including street name and name of a city or town;

(C) an e-mail address;

(D) a telephone number;

(E) a Social Security number;

(F) any other identifier that the Commission determines permits the physical or online contacting of a specific individual; or

(G) information concerning the child or the parents of that child that the website collects online from the child and combines with an identifier described in this paragraph.

(9) VERIFIABLE PARENTAL CONSENT.—The term "verifiable parental consent" means any reasonable effort (taking into consideration available technology), including a request for authorization for future collection, use, and disclosure described in the notice, to ensure that a parent of a child receives notice of the operator's personal information collection, use, and disclosure practices, and authorizes the collection, use, and disclosure, as applicable, of personal information and the subsequent use of that information before that information is collected from that child.

(10) WEBSITE OR ONLINE SERVICE DIRECTED TO CHILDREN.—

(A) IN GENERAL.—The term "website or online service directed to children" means—

(i) a commercial website or online service that is targeted to children; or

(ii) that portion of a commercial website or online service that is targeted to children.

(B) LIMITATION.—A commercial website or online service, or a portion of a commercial website or online service, shall not be deemed directed to children solely for referring or linking to a commercial website or online service directed to children by using information location tools, including a directory, index, reference, pointer, or hypertext link.

(11) PERSON.—The term "person" means any individual, partnership, corporation, trust, estate, cooperative, association, or other entity.

(12) ONLINE CONTACT INFORMATION.—The term "online contact information" means an e-mail address or another substantially similar identifier that permits direct contact with a person online.

SEC. 1303. REGULATION OF UNFAIR AND DECEPTIVE ACTS AND PRACTICES IN CONNECTION WITH THE COLLECTION AND USE OF PERSONAL INFORMATION FROM AND ABOUT CHILDREN ON THE INTERNET.

(a) ACTS PROHIBITED.—

(1) IN GENERAL.—It is unlawful for an operator of a website or on-line service directed to children, or any operator that has actual knowledge that it is collecting personal information from a child, to collect personal information from a child in a manner that violates the regulations prescribed under subsection (b).

(2) DISCLOSURE TO PARENT PROTECTED.—Notwithstanding paragraph (1), neither an operator of such a website or online service nor the operator's agent shall be held to be liable under any Federal or State law for any disclosure made in good faith and following reasonable procedures in responding to a request for disclosure of personal information under subsection (b)(1)(B)(iii) to the parent of a child.

(b) REGULATIONS.—

(1) IN GENERAL.—Not later than 1 year after the date of the enactment of this Act, the Commission shall promulgate under section 553 of title 5, United States Code, regulations that—

(A) require the operator of any website or online service directed to children that collects personal information from children or the operator of a website or online service that has actual knowledge that it is collecting personal information from a child—

(i) to provide notice on the website of what information is collected from children by the operator, how the operator uses such information, and the operator's disclosure practices for such information; and

(ii) to obtain verifiable parental consent for the collection, use, or disclosure of personal information from children;

(B) require the operator to provide, upon request of a parent under this subparagraph whose child has provided personal information to that website or online service, upon proper identification of that parent, to such parent—

(i) a description of the specific types of personal information collected from the child by that operator;

(ii) the opportunity at any time to refuse to permit the operator's further use or maintenance in retrievable form, or future online collection, of personal information from that child; and

(iii) notwithstanding any other provision of law, a means that is reasonable under the circumstances for the parent to obtain any personal information collected from that child;

(C) prohibit conditioning a child's participation in a game, the offering of a prize, or another activity on the child disclosing more personal information than is reasonably necessary to participate in such activity; and

(D) require the operator of such a website or online service to establish and maintain reasonable procedures to protect the confidentiality, security, and integrity of personal information collected from children.

(2) WHEN CONSENT NOT REQUIRED.—The regulations shall provide that verifiable parental consent under paragraph (1)(A)(ii) is not required in the case of—

(A) online contact information collected from a child that is used only to respond directly on a one-time basis to a specific request from the child and is not used to recontact the child and is not maintained in retrievable form by the operator;

(B) a request for the name or online contact information of a parent or child that is used for the sole purpose of obtaining parental consent or providing notice under this section and where such information is not maintained in retrievable form by the operator if parental consent is not obtained after a reasonable time;

(C) online contact information collected from a child that is used only to respond more than once directly to a specific request from the child and is not used to recontact the child beyond the scope of that request—

(i) if, before any additional response after the initial response to the child, the operator uses reasonable efforts to provide a parent notice of the online contact information collected from the child, the purposes for which it is to be used, and an opportunity for the parent to request that the operator make no further use of the information and that it not be maintained in retrievable form; or

(ii) without notice to the parent in such circumstances as the Commission may determine are appropriate, taking into consideration the benefits to the child of access to information and services, and risks to the security and privacy of the child, in regulations promulgated under this subsection;

(D) the name of the child and online contact information (to the extent reasonably necessary to protect the safety of a child participant on the site)—

(i) used only for the purpose of protecting such safety;

(ii) not used to recontact the child or for any other purpose; and

(iii) not disclosed on the site, if the operator uses reasonable efforts to provide a parent notice of the name and online contact information collected from the child, the purposes for which it is to be used, and an opportunity for the parent to request that the operator make no further use of the information and that it not be maintained in retrievable form; or

(E) the collection, use, or dissemination of such information by the operator of such a website or online service necessary—

(i) to protect the security or integrity of its website;

(ii) to take precautions against liability;

(iii) to respond to judicial process; or

(iv) to the extent permitted under other provisions of law, to provide information to law enforcement agencies or for an investigation on a matter related to public safety.

(3) TERMINATION OF SERVICE.—The regulations shall permit the operator of a website or an online service to terminate service provided to a child whose parent has refused, under the regulations prescribed under paragraph (1)(B)(ii), to permit the operator's further use or maintenance in retrievable form, or future online collection, of personal information from that child.

(c) ENFORCEMENT.—Subject to sections 1304 and 1306, a violation of a regulation prescribed under subsection (a) shall be treated as a violation of a rule defining an unfair or deceptive act or practice prescribed under section 18(a)(1)(B) of the Federal Trade Commission Act (15 U.S.C. § 57a(a)(1)(B)).

(d) INCONSISTENT STATE LAW.—No State or local government may impose any liability for commercial activities or actions by operators in interstate or foreign commerce in connection with an activity or action described in this title that is inconsistent with the treatment of those activities or actions under this section.

SEC. 1304. SAFE HARBORS.

(a) GUIDELINES.—An operator may satisfy the requirements of regulations issued under section 1303(b) by following a set of self-regulatory guidelines, issued by representatives of the marketing or online industries, or by other persons, approved under subsection (b).

(b) INCENTIVES.—

(1) SELF-REGULATORY INCENTIVES.—In prescribing regulations under section 1303, the Commission shall provide incentives for self-regulation by operators to implement the protections afforded children under the regulatory requirements described in subsection (b) of that section.

(2) DEEMED COMPLIANCE.—Such incentives shall include provisions for ensuring that a person will be deemed to be in compliance with the requirements of the regulations under section 1303 if that person complies with guidelines that, after notice and comment, are approved by the Commission upon making a determination that the guidelines meet the requirements of the regulations issued under section 1303.

(3) EXPEDITED RESPONSE TO REQUESTS.—The Commission shall act upon requests for safe harbor treatment within 180 days of the filing of the request, and shall set forth in writing its conclusions with regard to such requests.

(c) APPEALS.—Final action by the Commission on a request for approval of guidelines, or the failure to act within 180 days on a request for approval of guidelines, submitted under subsection (b) may be appealed to a district court of the United States of appropriate jurisdiction as provided for in section 706 of title 5, United States Code.

SEC. 1305. ACTIONS BY STATES.

(a) IN GENERAL.—

(1) CIVIL ACTIONS.—In any case in which the attorney general of a State has reason to believe that an interest of the residents of that State has been or is threatened or adversely affected by the engagement of any person in a practice that violates any regulation of the Commission prescribed under section 1303(b), the State, as parens patriae, may bring a civil action on behalf of the residents of the State in a district court of the United States of appropriate jurisdiction to—

(A) enjoin that practice;

(B) enforce compliance with the regulation;

(C) obtain damage, restitution, or other compensation on behalf of residents of the State; or

(D) obtain such other relief as the court may consider to be appropriate.

(2) NOTICE.—

(A) IN GENERAL.—Before filing an action under paragraph (1), the attorney general of the State involved shall provide to the Commission—

(i) written notice of that action; and

(ii) a copy of the complaint for that action.

(B) EXEMPTION.—

(i) IN GENERAL.—Subparagraph (A) shall not apply with respect to the filing of an action by an attorney general of a State under this subsection, if the attorney general determines that it is not feasible to provide the notice described in that subparagraph before the filing of the action.

(ii) NOTIFICATION.—In an action described in clause (i), the attorney general of a State shall provide notice and a copy of the complaint to the Commission at the same time as the attorney general files the action.

(b) INTERVENTION.—

(1) IN GENERAL.—On receiving notice under subsection (a)(2), the Commission shall have the right to intervene in the action that is the subject of the notice.

(2) EFFECT OF INTERVENTION.—If the Commission intervenes in an action under subsection (a), it shall have the right—

(A) to be heard with respect to any matter that arises in that action; and

(B) to file a petition for appeal.

(3) AMICUS CURIAE.—Upon application to the court, a person whose self-regulatory guidelines have been approved by the Commission and are relied upon as a defense by any defendant to a proceeding under this section may file amicus curiae in that proceeding.

(c) CONSTRUCTION.—For purposes of bringing any civil action under subsection (a), nothing in this title shall be construed to prevent an attorney general of a State from exercising the powers conferred on the attorney general by the laws of that State to—

(1) conduct investigations;

(2) administer oaths or affirmations; or

(3) compel the attendance of witnesses or the production of documentary and other evidence.

(d) ACTIONS BY THE COMMISSION.—In any case in which an action is instituted by or on behalf of the Commission for violation of any regulation prescribed under section 1303, no State may, during the pendency of that action, institute an action under subsection (a) against any defendant named in the complaint in that action for violation of that regulation.

(e) VENUE; SERVICE OF PROCESS.—

(1) VENUE.—Any action brought under subsection (a) may be brought in the district court of the United States that meets applicable requirements relating to venue under section 1391 of title 28, United States Code.

(2) SERVICE OF PROCESS.—In an action brought under subsection (a), process may be served in any district in which the defendant—

(A) is an inhabitant; or

(B) may be found.

SEC. 1306. ADMINISTRATION AND APPLICABILITY OF ACT.

(a) IN GENERAL.—Except as otherwise provided, this title shall be enforced by the Commission under the Federal Trade Commission Act (15 U.S.C. § 41 et seq.).

(b) PROVISIONS.—Compliance with the requirements imposed under this title shall be enforced under—

(1) section 8 of the Federal Deposit Insurance Act (12 U.S.C. § 1818), in the case of—

(A) national banks, and Federal branches and Federal agencies of foreign banks, by the Office of the Comptroller of the Currency;

(B) member banks of the Federal Reserve System (other than national banks), branches and agencies of foreign banks (other than Federal branches, Federal agencies, and insured State branches of foreign banks), commercial lending companies owned or controlled by foreign banks, and organizations operating under section 25 or 25(a) of the Federal Reserve Act (12 U.S.C. § 601 et seq. and 611 et seq.), by the Board; and

(C) banks insured by the Federal Deposit Insurance Corporation (other than members of the Federal Reserve System) and insured State branches of foreign banks, by the Board of Directors of the Federal Deposit Insurance Corporation;

(2) section 8 of the Federal Deposit Insurance Act (12 U.S.C. § 1818), by the Director of the Office of Thrift Supervision, in the case of a savings association the deposits of which are insured by the Federal Deposit Insurance Corporation;

(3) the Federal Credit Union Act (12 U.S.C. § 1751 et seq.) by the National Credit Union Administration Board with respect to any Federal credit union;

(4) part A of subtitle VII of title 49, United States Code, by the Secretary of Transportation with respect to any air carrier or foreign air carrier subject to that part;

(5) the Packers and Stockyards Act, 1921 (7 U.S.C. § 181 et seq.) (except as provided in section 406 of that Act (7 U.S.C. § 226, 227)), by the Secretary of Agriculture with respect to any activities subject to that Act; and

(6) the Farm Credit Act of 1971 (12 U.S.C. § 2001 et seq.) by the Farm Credit Administration with respect to any Federal land bank, Federal land bank association, Federal intermediate credit bank, or production credit association.

(c) EXERCISE OF CERTAIN POWERS.—For the purpose of the exercise by any agency referred to in subsection (a) of its powers under any Act referred to in that subsection, a violation of any requirement imposed under this title shall be deemed to be a violation of a requirement imposed under that Act. In addition to its powers under any provision of law specifically referred to in subsection (a), each of the agencies referred to in that subsection may exercise, for the purpose of enforcing compliance with any requirement imposed under this title, any other authority conferred on it by law.

(d) ACTIONS BY THE COMMISSION.—The Commission shall prevent any person from violating a rule of the Commission under section 1303 in the same manner, by the same means, and with the same jurisdiction, powers, and duties as though all applicable terms and provisions of the Federal Trade Commission Act (15 U.S.C. § 41 et seq.) were incorporated into and made a part of this title. Any entity that violates such rule shall be subject to the penalties and entitled to the privileges and immunities provided in the Federal Trade Commission Act in the same manner, by the same means, and with the same jurisdiction, power, and duties as though all applicable terms and provisions of the Federal Trade Commission Act were incorporated into and made a part of this title.

(e) EFFECT ON OTHER LAWS.—Nothing contained in the Act shall be construed to limit the authority of the Commission under any other provisions of law.

SEC. 1307. REVIEW.

Not later than 5 years after the effective date of the regulations initially issued under section 1303, the Commission shall—

(1) review the implementation of this title, including the effect of the implementation of this title on practices relating to the collection and disclosure of information relating to children, children's ability to obtain access to information of their choice online, and on the availability of websites directed to children; and

(2) prepare and submit to Congress a report on the results of the review under paragraph (1).

SEC. 1308. EFFECTIVE DATE.

Sections 1303(a), 1305, and 1306 of this title take effect on the later of—

(1) the date that is 18 months after the date of enactment of this Act; or

(2) the date on which the Commission rules on the first application filed for safe harbor treatment under section 1304 if the Commission does not rule on the first such application within one year after the date of enactment of this Act, but in no case later than the date that is 30 months after the date of enactment of this Act.

APPENDIX 16:
THE CHILDREN'S INTERNET PROTECTION ACT (PUBLIC LAW 106-554)

TITLE XVII—CHILDREN'S INTERNET PROTECTION

SEC. 1701. SHORT TITLE.

This title may be cited as the "Children's Internet Protection Act".

SEC. 1702. DISCLAIMERS.

(a) DISCLAIMER REGARDING CONTENT.—Nothing in this title or the amendments made by this title shall be construed to prohibit a local educational agency, elementary or secondary school, or library from blocking access on the Internet on computers owned or operated by that agency, school, or library to any content other than content covered by this title or the amendments made by this title.

(b) DISCLAIMER REGARDING PRIVACY.—Nothing in this title or the amendments made by this title shall be construed to require the tracking of Internet use by any identifiable minor or adult user.

SEC. 1703. STUDY OF TECHNOLOGY PROTECTION MEASURES.

IN GENERAL.—Not later than 18 months after the date of the enactment of this Act, the National Telecommunications and Information Administration shall initiate a notice and comment proceeding for purposes of—

(1) evaluating whether or not currently available technology protection measures, including commercial Internet blocking and filtering software, adequately addresses the needs of educational institutions;

(2) making recommendations on how to foster the development of measures that meet such needs; and

(3) evaluating the development and effectiveness of local Internet safety policies that are currently in operation after community input.

DEFINITIONS.—In this section:

TECHNOLOGY PROTECTION MEASURE.—The term "technology protection measure" means a specific technology that blocks or filters Internet access to visual depictions that are—

(A) obscene, as that term is defined in section 1460 of title 18, United States Code;

(B) child pornography, as that term is defined in section 2256 of title 18, United States Code; or

(C) harmful to minors.

(2) HARMFUL TO MINORS.—The term "harmful to minors" means any picture, image, graphic image file, or other visual depiction that—

(A) taken as a whole and with respect to minors, appeals to a prurient interest in nudity, sex, or excretion;

(B) depicts, describes, or represents, in a patently offensive way with respect to what is suitable for minors, an actual or simulated sexual act or sexual contact, actual or simulated normal or perverted sexual acts, or a lewd exhibition of the genitals; and

(C) taken as a whole, lacks serious literary, artistic, political, or scientific value as to minors.

(3) SEXUAL ACT; SEXUAL CONTACT.—The terms "sexual act" and "sexual contact" have the meanings given such terms in section 2246 of title 18, United States Code.

SUBTITLE A—FEDERAL FUNDING FOR EDUCATIONAL INSTITUTION COMPUTERS

SEC. 1711. LIMITATION ON AVAILABILITY OF CERTAIN FUNDS FOR SCHOOLS.

Title III of the Elementary and Secondary Education Act of 1965 (20 U.S.C. 6801 et seq.) is amended by adding at the end the following:

"PART F—LIMITATION ON AVAILABILITY OF CERTAIN FUNDS FOR SCHOOLS

"SEC. 3601. LIMITATION ON AVAILABILITY OF CERTAIN FUNDS FOR SCHOOLS.

"(a) INTERNET SAFETY.—

"(1) IN GENERAL.—No funds made available under this title to a local educational agency for an elementary or secondary school that does not receive services at discount rates under section 254(h)(5) of the Communications Act of 1934, as added by section 1721 of Children's Internet Protection Act, may be used to purchase computers used to access the Internet, or to pay for direct costs associated with accessing the Internet, for such school unless the school, school board, local educational agency, or other authority with responsibility for administration of such school both—

"(A)(i) has in place a policy of Internet safety for minors that includes the operation of a technology protection measure with respect to any of its computers with Internet access that protects against access through such computers to visual depictions that are—

"(I) obscene;

"(II) child pornography; or

"(III) harmful to minors; and

"(ii) is enforcing the operation of such technology protection measure during any use of such computers by minors; and

"(B)(i) has in place a policy of Internet safety that includes the operation of a technology protection measure with respect to any of its computers with Internet access that protects against access through such computers to visual depictions that are—

"(I) obscene; or

"(II) child pornography; and

"(ii) is enforcing the operation of such technology protection measure during any use of such computers.

"(2) TIMING AND APPLICABILITY OF IMPLEMENTATION.—

"(A) IN GENERAL.—The local educational agency with responsibility for a school covered by paragraph (1) shall certify the compliance of such school with the requirements of paragraph (1) as part of the application process for the next program funding year under this Act following the effective date of this section, and for each subsequent program funding year thereafter.

"(B) PROCESS.—

"(i) SCHOOLS WITH INTERNET SAFETY POLICIES AND TECHNOLOGY PROTECTION MEASURES IN PLACE.—A local educational agency with responsibility for a school covered by paragraph (1) that has in place an Internet safety policy meeting the requirements of paragraph (1) shall certify its compliance with paragraph (1) during each annual program application cycle under this Act.

"(ii) SCHOOLS WITHOUT INTERNET SAFETY POLICIES AND TECHNOLOGY PROTECTION MEASURES IN PLACE.—A local educational agency with responsibility for a school covered by paragraph (1) that does not have in place an Internet safety policy meeting the requirements of paragraph (1)—

"(I) for the first program year after the effective date of this section in which the local educational agency is applying for funds for such school under this Act, shall certify that it is undertaking such actions, including any necessary procurement procedures, to put in place an Internet safety policy that meets such requirements; and

"(II) for the second program year after the effective date of this section in which the local educational agency is applying for funds for such school under this Act, shall certify that such school is in compliance with such requirements.

Any school covered by paragraph (1) for which the local educational agency concerned is unable to certify compliance with such requirements in such second program year shall be ineligible for all funding under this title for such second program year and all subsequent program years until such time as such school comes into compliance with such requirements.

"(iii) WAIVERS.—Any school subject to a certification under clause (ii)(II) for which the local educational agency concerned cannot make the certification otherwise required by that clause may seek a waiver of that clause if State or local procurement rules or regulations or competitive bidding requirements prevent the making of the certification otherwise required by that clause. The local educational agency concerned shall notify the Secretary of the applicability of that clause to the school. Such notice shall certify that the school will be brought into compliance with the requirements in paragraph (1) before the start of the third program year after the effective date of this section in which the school is applying for funds under this title.

"(3) DISABLING DURING CERTAIN USE.—An administrator, supervisor, or person authorized by the responsible authority under paragraph (1) may disable the technology protection measure concerned to enable access for bona fide research or other lawful purposes.

"(4) NONCOMPLIANCE.—

"(A) USE OF GENERAL EDUCATION PROVISIONS ACT REMEDIES.—Whenever the Secretary has reason to believe that any recipient of funds under this title is failing to comply substantially with the requirements of this subsection, the Secretary may—

"(i) withhold further payments to the recipient under this title,

"(ii) issue a complaint to compel compliance of the recipient through a cease and desist order, or

"(iii) enter into a compliance agreement with a recipient to bring it into compliance with such requirements, in same manner as the Secretary is authorized to take such actions under sections 455, 456, and 457, respectively, of the General Education Provisions Act (20 U.S.C. 1234d).

"(B) RECOVERY OF FUNDS PROHIBITED.—The actions authorized

by subparagraph (A) are the exclusive remedies available with respect to the failure of a school to comply substantially with a provision of this subsection, and the Secretary shall not seek a recovery of funds from the recipient for such failure.

"(C) RECOMMENCEMENT OF PAYMENTS.—Whenever the Secretary determines (whether by certification or other appropriate evidence) that a recipient of funds who is subject to the withholding of payments under subparagraph (A)(i) has cured the failure providing the basis for the withholding of payments, the Secretary shall cease the withholding of payments to the recipient under that subparagraph.

"(5) DEFINITIONS.—In this section:

"(A) COMPUTER.—The term 'computer' includes any hardware, software, or other technology attached or connected to, installed in, or otherwise used in connection with a computer.

"(B) ACCESS TO INTERNET.—A computer shall be considered to have access to the Internet if such computer is equipped with a modem or is connected to a computer network which has access to the Internet.

"(C) ACQUISITION OR OPERATION.—A elementary or secondary school shall be considered to have received funds under this title for the acquisition or operation of any computer if such funds are used in any manner, directly or indirectly—

"(i) to purchase, lease, or otherwise acquire or obtain the use of such computer; or

"(ii) to obtain services, supplies, software, or other actions or materials to support, or in connection with, the operation of such computer.

"(D) MINOR.—The term 'minor' means an individual who has not attained the age of 17.

"(E) CHILD PORNOGRAPHY.—The term 'child pornography' has the meaning given such term in section 2256 of title 18, United States Code.

"(F) HARMFUL TO MINORS.—The term 'harmful to minors' means any picture, image, graphic image file, or other visual depiction that—

"(i) taken as a whole and with respect to minors, appeals to a prurient interest in nudity, sex, or excretion;

"(ii) depicts, describes, or represents, in a patently offensive way with respect to what is suitable for minors, an actual or simulated sexual act or sexual contact, actual or simulated normal or perverted sexual acts, or a lewd exhibition of the genitals; and

"(iii) taken as a whole, lacks serious literary, artistic, political, or scientific value as to minors.

"(G) OBSCENE.—The term 'obscene' has the meaning given such term in section 1460 of title 18, United States Code.

"(H) SEXUAL ACT; SEXUAL CONTACT.—The terms 'sexual act' and 'sexual contact' have the meanings given such terms in section 2246 of title 18, United States Code.

"(b) EFFECTIVE DATE.—This section shall take effect 120 days after the date of the enactment of the Children's Internet Protection Act.

"(c) SEPARABILITY.—If any provision of this section is held invalid, the remainder of this section shall not be affected thereby."

SEC. 1712. LIMITATION ON AVAILABILITY OF CERTAIN FUNDS FOR LIBRARIES.

AMENDMENT.—Section 224 of the Museum and Library Services Act (20 U.S.C. 9134(b)) is amended—

(1) in subsection (b)—

(A) by redesignating paragraph (6) as paragraph (7); and

(B) by inserting after paragraph (5) the following new paragraph:

"(6) provide assurances that the State will comply with subsection (f); and"; and by adding at the end the following new subsection:

"(f) INTERNET SAFETY.—

"(1) IN GENERAL.—No funds made available under this Act for a library described in section 213(2)(A) or (B) that does not receive services at discount rates under section 254(h)(6) of the Communications Act of 1934, as added by section 1721 of this Children's Internet Protection Act, may be used to purchase computers used to access the Internet, or to pay for direct costs associated with accessing the Internet, for such library unless—

"(A) such library—

"(i) has in place a policy of Internet safety for minors that includes the operation of a technology protection measure with respect to any of its computers with Internet access that protects against access through such computers to visual depictions that are—

"(I) obscene;

"(II) child pornography; or

"(III) harmful to minors; and

"(ii) is enforcing the operation of such technology protection measure during any use of such computers by minors; and

"(B) such library—

"(i) has in place a policy of Internet safety that includes the operation of a technology protection measure with respect to any of its computers with Internet access that protects against access through such computers to visual depictions that are—

"(I) obscene; or

"(II) child pornography; and

"(ii) is enforcing the operation of such technology protection measure during any use of such computers.

"(2) ACCESS TO OTHER MATERIALS.—Nothing in this subsection shall be construed to prohibit a library from limiting Internet access to or otherwise protecting against materials other than those referred to in subclauses (I), (II), and (III) of paragraph (1)(A)(i).

"(3) DISABLING DURING CERTAIN USE.—An administrator, supervisor, or other authority may disable a technology protection measure under paragraph (1) to enable access for bona fide research or other lawful purposes.

"(4) TIMING AND APPLICABILITY OF IMPLEMENTATION.—

"(A) IN GENERAL.—A library covered by paragraph (1) shall certify the compliance of such library with the requirements of paragraph (1) as part of the application process for the next program funding year under this Act following the effective date of this subsection, and for each subsequent program funding year thereafter.

"(B) PROCESS.—

"(i) LIBRARIES WITH INTERNET SAFETY POLICIES AND TECHNOLOGY PROTECTION MEASURES IN PLACE.—A library covered by paragraph (1) that has in place an Internet safety policy meeting the requirements of paragraph (1) shall certify its compliance with paragraph (1) during each annual program application cycle under this Act.

"(ii) LIBRARIES WITHOUT INTERNET SAFETY POLICIES AND TECHNOLOGY PROTECTION MEASURES IN PLACE.—A library covered by paragraph (1) that does not have in place an Internet safety policy meeting the requirements of paragraph (1)—

"(I) for the first program year after the effective date of this subsection in which the library applies for funds under this Act, shall certify that it is undertaking such actions, including any necessary procurement procedures, to put in place an Internet safety policy that meets such requirements; and

"(II) for the second program year after the effective date of this subsection in which the library applies for funds under this Act, shall certify that such library is in compliance with such requirements.

Any library covered by paragraph (1) that is unable to certify compliance with such requirements in such second program year shall be ineligible for all funding under this Act for such second program year and all subsequent program years until such time as such library comes into compliance with such requirements.

"(iii) WAIVERS.—Any library subject to a certification under clause (ii)(II) that cannot make the certification otherwise required by that clause may seek a waiver of that clause if State or local procurement rules or regulations or competitive bidding requirements prevent the making of the certification otherwise required by that clause. The library shall notify the Director of the Institute of Museum and Library Services of the applicability of that clause to the library. Such notice shall certify that the library will comply with the requirements in paragraph (1) before the start of the third program year after the effective date of this subsection for which the library is applying for funds under this Act.

"(5) NONCOMPLIANCE.—

"(A) USE OF GENERAL EDUCATION PROVISIONS ACT REMEDIES.—Whenever the Director of the Institute of Museum and Library Services has reason to believe that any recipient of funds this Act is failing to comply substantially with the requirements of this subsection, the Director may—

"(i) withhold further payments to the recipient under this Act,

"(ii) issue a complaint to compel compliance of the recipient through a cease and desist order, or

"(iii) enter into a compliance agreement with a recipient to bring it into compliance with such requirements.

"(B) RECOVERY OF FUNDS PROHIBITED.—The actions authorized by subparagraph (A) are the exclusive remedies available with respect to the failure of a library to comply substantially with a provision of this subsection, and the Director shall not seek a recovery of funds from the recipient for such failure.

"(C) RECOMMENCEMENT OF PAYMENTS.—Whenever the Director determines (whether by certification or other appropriate evidence) that a recipient of funds who is subject to the withholding of payments under subparagraph (A)(i) has cured the failure providing the basis for the withholding of payments, the Director shall cease the withholding of payments to the recipient under that subparagraph.

"(6) SEPARABILITY.—If any provision of this subsection is held invalid, the remainder of this subsection shall not be affected thereby.

"(7) DEFINITIONS.—In this section:

"(A) CHILD PORNOGRAPHY.—The term 'child pornography' has the meaning given such term in section 2256 of title 18, United States Code.

"(B) HARMFUL TO MINORS.—The term 'harmful to minors' means any picture, image, graphic image file, or other visual depiction that—

"(i) taken as a whole and with respect to minors, appeals to a prurient interest in nudity, sex, or excretion;

"(ii) depicts, describes, or represents, in a patently offensive way with respect to what is suitable for minors, an actual or simulated sexual act or sexual contact, actual or simulated normal or perverted sexual acts, or a lewd exhibition of the genitals; and

"(iii) taken as a whole, lacks serious literary, artistic, political, or scientific value as to minors.

"(C) MINOR.—The term 'minor' means an individual who has not attained the age of 17.

"(D) OBSCENE.—The term 'obscene' has the meaning given such term in section 1460 of title 18, United States Code.

"(E) SEXUAL ACT; SEXUAL CONTACT.—The terms 'sexual act' and 'sexual contact' have the meanings given such terms in section 2246 of title 18, United States Code."

EFFECTIVE DATE.—The amendment made by this section shall take effect 120 days after the date of the enactment of this Act.

SUBTITLE B—UNIVERSAL SERVICE DISCOUNTS

SEC. 1721. REQUIREMENT FOR SCHOOLS AND LIBRARIES TO ENFORCE INTERNET SAFETY POLICIES WITH TECHNOLOGY PROTECTION MEASURES FOR COMPUTERS WITH INTERNET ACCESS AS CONDITION OF UNIVERSAL SERVICE DISCOUNTS.

SCHOOLS.—Section 254(h) of the Communications Act of 1934 (47 U.S.C. 254(h)) is amended—

(1) by re-designating paragraph (5) as paragraph (7); and by inserting after paragraph (4) the following new paragraph (5):

"(5) REQUIREMENTS FOR CERTAIN SCHOOLS WITH COMPUTERS HAVING INTERNET ACCESS.—

"(A) INTERNET SAFETY.—

"(i) IN GENERAL.—Except as provided in clause (ii), an elementary or secondary school having computers with Internet access may not receive services at discount rates under paragraph (1)(B) unless the school, school board, local educational agency, or other authority with responsibility for administration of the school—

"(I) submits to the Commission the certifications described in subparagraphs (B) and (C);

"(II) submits to the Commission a certification that an Internet safety policy has been adopted and implemented for the school under subsection (l); and

"(III) ensures the use of such computers in accordance with the certifications.

"(ii) APPLICABILITY.—The prohibition in clause (i) shall not apply with respect to a school that receives services at discount rates under paragraph (1)(B) only for purposes other than the provision of Internet access, Internet service, or internal connections.

"(iii) PUBLIC NOTICE; HEARING.—An elementary or secondary school described in clause (i), or the school board, local educational agency, or other authority with responsibility for administration of the school, shall provide reasonable public notice and hold at least 1 public hearing or meeting to address the proposed Internet safety policy. In the case of an elementary or secondary school other than an elementary or secondary school as defined in section 14101 of the Elementary and Secondary Education Act of 1965 (20 U.S.C. 8801), the notice and hearing required by this clause may be limited to those members of the public with a relationship to the school.

"(B) CERTIFICATION WITH RESPECT TO MINORS.—A certification under this subparagraph is a certification that the school, school board, local educational agency, or other authority with responsibility for administration of the school—

"(i) is enforcing a policy of Internet safety for minors that includes monitoring the online activities of minors and the operation of a technology protection measure with respect to any of its computers with Internet access that protects against access through such computers to visual depictions that are—

"(I) obscene;

"(II) child pornography; or

"(III) harmful to minors; and

"(ii) is enforcing the operation of such technology protection measure during any use of such computers by minors.

"(C) CERTIFICATION WITH RESPECT TO ADULTS.—A certification under this paragraph is a certification that the school, school board, local educational agency, or other authority with responsibility for administration of the school—

"(i) is enforcing a policy of Internet safety that includes the operation of a technology protection measure with respect to any of its computers with Internet access that protects against access through such computers to visual depictions that are—

"(I) obscene; or

"(II) child pornography; and

"(ii) is enforcing the operation of such technology protection measure during any use of such computers.

"(D) DISABLING DURING ADULT USE.—An administrator, supervisor, or other person authorized by the certifying authority under subparagraph (A)(i) may disable the technology protection measure concerned, during use by an adult, to enable access for bona fide research or other lawful purpose.

"(E) TIMING OF IMPLEMENTATION.—

"(i) IN GENERAL.—Subject to clause (ii) in the case of any school covered by this paragraph as of the effective date of this paragraph under section 1721(h) of the Children's Internet

Protection Act, the certification under subparagraphs (B) and (C) shall be made—

"(I) with respect to the first program funding year under this subsection following such effective date, not later than 120 days after the beginning of such program funding year; and

"(II) with respect to any subsequent program funding year, as part of the application process for such program funding year.

"(ii) PROCESS.—

"(I) SCHOOLS WITH INTERNET SAFETY POLICY AND TECH-NOLOGY PROTECTION MEASURES IN PLACE.—A school covered by clause (i) that has in place an Internet safety policy and technology protection measures meeting the requirements necessary for certification under subparagraphs (B) and (C) shall certify its compliance with subparagraphs (B) and (C) during each annual program application cycle under this subsection, except that with respect to the first program funding year after the effective date of this paragraph under section 1721(h) of the Children's Internet Protection Act, the certifications shall be made not later than 120 days after the beginning of such first program funding year.

"(II) SCHOOLS WITHOUT INTERNET SAFETY POLICY AND TECHNOLOGY PROTECTION MEASURES IN PLACE.—A school covered by clause (i) that does not have in place an Internet safety policy and technology protection measures meeting the requirements necessary for certification under subparagraphs (B) and (C)—

"(aa) for the first program year after the effective date of this subsection in which it is applying for funds under this subsection, shall certify that it is undertaking such actions, including any necessary procurement procedures, to put in place an Internet safety policy and technology protection measures meeting the requirements necessary for certification under subparagraphs (B) and (C); and

"(bb) for the second program year after the effective date of this subsection in which it is applying for funds under this subsection, shall certify that it is in compliance with subparagraphs (B) and (C).

Any school that is unable to certify compliance with such requirements in such second program year shall be ineligible for services at discount rates or funding in lieu of services at such rates under this subsection for such second year and all subsequent program years under this subsection, until such time as such school comes into compliance with this paragraph.

"(III) WAIVERS.—Any school subject to subclause (II) that cannot come into compliance with subparagraphs (B) and (C) in such second year program may seek a waiver of subclause (II)(bb) if State or local procurement rules or regulations or competitive bidding requirements prevent the making of the certification otherwise required by such subclause. A school, school board, local educational agency, or other authority with responsibility for administration of the school shall notify the Commission of the applicability of such subclause to the school. Such notice shall certify that the school in question will be brought into compliance before the start of the third program year after the effective date of this subsection in which the school is applying for funds under this subsection.

"(F) NONCOMPLIANCE.—

"(i) FAILURE TO SUBMIT CERTIFICATION.—Any school that knowingly fails to comply with the application guidelines regarding the annual submission of certification required by this paragraph shall not be eligible for services at discount rates or funding in lieu of services at such rates under this subsection.

"(ii) FAILURE TO COMPLY WITH CERTIFICATION.—Any school that knowingly fails to ensure the use of its computers in accordance with a certification under subparagraphs (B) and (C) shall reimburse any funds and discounts received under this subsection for the period covered by such certification.

"(iii) REMEDY OF NONCOMPLIANCE.—

"(I) FAILURE TO SUBMIT.—A school that has failed to submit a certification under clause (i) may remedy the failure by submitting the certification to which the failure relates. Upon submittal of such certification, the school shall be eligible for services at discount rates under this subsection.

"(II) FAILURE TO COMPLY.—A school that has failed to comply with a certification as described in clause (ii) may remedy the failure by ensuring the use of its computers in accordance with such certification. Upon submittal to the Commission of a certification or other appropriate evidence of such remedy, the school shall be eligible for services at discount rates under this subsection.".

LIBRARIES.—Such section 254(h) is further amended by inserting after paragraph (5), as amended by subsection (a) of this section, the following new paragraph:

"(6) REQUIREMENTS FOR CERTAIN LIBRARIES WITH COMPUTERS HAVING INTERNET ACCESS.—

"(A) INTERNET SAFETY.—

"(i) IN GENERAL.—Except as provided in clause (ii), a library having one or more computers with Internet access may not receive services at discount rates under paragraph (1)(B) unless the library—

"(I) submits to the Commission the certifications described in subparagraphs (B) and (C); and

"(II) submits to the Commission a certification that an Internet safety policy has been adopted and implemented for the library under subsection (l); and

"(III) ensures the use of such computers in accordance with the certifications.

"(ii) APPLICABILITY.—The prohibition in clause (i) shall not apply with respect to a library that receives services at discount rates under paragraph (1)(B) only for purposes other than the provision of Internet access, Internet service, or internal connections.

"(iii) PUBLIC NOTICE; HEARING.—A library described in clause (i) shall provide reasonable public notice and hold at least 1 public hearing or meeting to address the proposed Internet safety policy.

"(B) CERTIFICATION WITH RESPECT TO MINORS.—A certification under this subparagraph is a certification that the library—

"(i) is enforcing a policy of Internet safety that includes the operation of a technology protection measure with respect to any of its computers with Internet access that protects against access through such computers to visual depictions that are—

"(I) obscene;

"(II) child pornography; or

"(III) harmful to minors; and

"(ii) is enforcing the operation of such technology protection measure during any use of such computers by minors.

"(C) CERTIFICATION WITH RESPECT TO ADULTS.—A certification under this paragraph is a certification that the library—

"(i) is enforcing a policy of Internet safety that includes the operation of a technology protection measure with respect to any of its computers with Internet access that protects against access through such computers to visual depictions that are—

"(I) obscene; or

"(II) child pornography; and

"(ii) is enforcing the operation of such technology protection measure during any use of such computers.

"(D) DISABLING DURING ADULT USE.—An administrator, supervisor, or other person authorized by the certifying authority under subparagraph (A)(i) may disable the technology protection measure concerned, during use by an adult, to enable access for bona fide research or other lawful purpose.

"(E) TIMING OF IMPLEMENTATION.—

"(i) IN GENERAL.—Subject to clause (ii) in the case of any library covered by this paragraph as of the effective date of this paragraph under section 1721(h) of the Children's Internet Protection Act, the certification under subparagraphs (B) and (C) shall be made—

"(I) with respect to the first program funding year under this subsection following such effective date, not later than 120 days after the beginning of such program funding year; and

"(II) with respect to any subsequent program funding year, as part of the application process for such program funding year.

"(ii) PROCESS.—

"(I) LIBRARIES WITH INTERNET SAFETY POLICY AND TECHNOLOGY PROTECTION MEASURES IN PLACE.—A library covered by clause (i) that has in place an Internet safety policy and technology protection measures meeting the requirements necessary for certification under subparagraphs (B) and (C) shall certify its compliance with subparagraphs (B) and (C) during each annual program application cycle under this subsection, except that with respect to the first program funding year after the effective date of this paragraph under section 1721(h) of the Children's Internet Protection Act, the certifications shall be made not later than 120 days after the beginning of such first program funding year.

"(II) LIBRARIES WITHOUT INTERNET SAFETY POLICY AND TECHNOLOGY PROTECTION MEASURES IN PLACE.—A library covered by clause (i) that does not have in place an Internet safety policy and technology protection measures meeting the requirements necessary for certification under subparagraphs (B) and (C)—

"(aa) for the first program year after the effective date of this subsection in which it is applying for funds under this subsection, shall certify that it is undertaking such actions, including any necessary procurement procedures, to put in place an Internet safety policy and technology protection measures meeting the requirements necessary for certification under subparagraphs (B) and (C); and

"(bb) for the second program year after the effective date of this subsection in which it is applying for funds under this subsection, shall certify that it is in compliance with subparagraphs (B) and (C).

Any library that is unable to certify compliance with such requirements in such second program year shall be ineligible for services at discount rates or funding in lieu of services at such rates under this subsection for such second year and all subsequent program years under this subsection, until such time as such library comes into compliance with this paragraph.

"(III) WAIVERS.—Any library subject to subclause (II) that cannot come into compliance with subparagraphs (B) and (C) in such second year may seek a waiver of subclause (II)(bb) if State or local procurement rules or regulations or competitive bidding requirements prevent the making of the certification otherwise required by such subclause. A library, library board, or other authority with responsibility for administration of the library shall notify the Commission of the applicability of such subclause to the library. Such notice shall certify that the library in question will be brought into compliance before the start of the third program year after the effective date of this subsection in which the library is applying for funds under this subsection.

"(F) NONCOMPLIANCE.—

"(i) FAILURE TO SUBMIT CERTIFICATION.—Any library that knowingly fails to comply with the application guidelines regarding the annual submission of certification required by this paragraph shall not be eligible for services at discount rates or funding in lieu of services at such rates under this subsection.

"(ii) FAILURE TO COMPLY WITH CERTIFICATION.—Any library that knowingly fails to ensure the use of its computers in accordance with a certification under subparagraphs (B) and (C) shall reimburse all funds and discounts received under this subsection for the period covered by such certification.

"(iii) REMEDY OF NONCOMPLIANCE.—

"(I) FAILURE TO SUBMIT.—A library that has failed to submit a certification under clause (i) may remedy the failure by submitting the certification to which the failure relates. Upon submittal of such certification, the library shall be eligible for services at discount rates under this subsection.

"(II) FAILURE TO COMPLY.—A library that has failed to comply with a certification as described in clause (ii) may remedy the failure by ensuring the use of its computers in accordance with such certification. Upon submittal to the Commission of a certification or other appropriate evidence of such remedy, the library shall be eligible for services at discount rates under this subsection.".

DEFINITIONS.—Paragraph (7) of such section, as redesignated by subsection (a)(1) of this section, is amended by adding at the end the following:

"(D) MINOR.—The term 'minor' means any individual who has not attained the age of 17 years.

"(E) OBSCENE.—The term 'obscene' has the meaning given such term in section 1460 of title 18, United States Code.

"(F) CHILD PORNOGRAPHY.—The term 'child pornography' has the meaning given such term in section 2256 of title 18, United States Code.

"(G) HARMFUL TO MINORS.—The term 'harmful to minors' means any picture, image, graphic image file, or other visual depiction that—

"(i) taken as a whole and with respect to minors, appeals to a prurient interest in nudity, sex, or excretion;

"(ii) depicts, describes, or represents, in a patently offensive way with respect to what is suitable for minors, an actual or simulated sexual act or sexual contact, actual or simulated normal or perverted sexual acts, or a lewd exhibition of the genitals; and

"(iii) taken as a whole, lacks serious literary, artistic, political, or scientific value as to minors.

"(H) SEXUAL ACT; SEXUAL CONTACT.—The terms 'sexual act' and 'sexual contact' have the meanings given such terms in section 2246 of title 18, United States Code.

"(I) TECHNOLOGY PROTECTION MEASURE.—The term 'technology protection measure' means a specific technology that blocks or filters Internet access to the material covered by a certification under paragraph (5) or (6) to which such certification relates.".

(d) CONFORMING AMENDMENT.—Paragraph (4) of such section is amended by striking "paragraph (5)(A)" and inserting "paragraph (7)(A)".

(e) SEPARABILITY.—If any provision of paragraph (5) or (6) of section 254(h) of the Communications Act of 1934, as amended by this section, or the application thereof to any person or circumstance is held invalid, the remainder of such paragraph and the application of such paragraph to other persons or circumstances shall not be affected thereby.

(f) REGULATIONS.—

(1) REQUIREMENT.—The Federal Communications Commission shall prescribe regulations for purposes of administering the provisions of paragraphs (5) and (6) of section 254(h) of the Communications Act of 1934, as amended by this section.

(2) DEADLINE.—Notwithstanding any other provision of law, the Commission shall prescribe regulations under paragraph (1) so as to ensure that such regulations take effect 120 days after the date of the enactment of this Act.

(g) AVAILABILITY OF CERTAIN FUNDS FOR ACQUISITION OF TECHNOLOGY PROTECTION MEASURES.—

(1) IN GENERAL.—Notwithstanding any other provision of law, funds available under section 3134 or part A of title VI of the Elementary and Secondary Education Act of 1965, or under section 231 of the Library Services and Technology Act, may be used for the purchase or acquisition of technology protection measures that are necessary to meet the requirements of this title and the amendments made by this title. No other sources of funds for the purchase or acquisition of such measures are authorized by this title, or the amendments made by this title.

(2) TECHNOLOGY PROTECTION MEASURE DEFINED.—In this section, the term "technology protection measure" has the meaning given that term in section 1703.

(h) EFFECTIVE DATE.—The amendments made by this section shall take effect 120 days after the date of the enactment of this Act.

SUBTITLE C—NEIGHBORHOOD CHILDREN'S INTERNET PROTECTION

SEC. 1731. SHORT TITLE.

This subtitle may be cited as the "Neighborhood Children's Internet Protection Act".

SEC. 1732. INTERNET SAFETY POLICY REQUIRED.

Section 254 of the Communications Act of 1934 (47 U.S.C. 254) is amended by adding at the end the following:

"(l) INTERNET SAFETY POLICY REQUIREMENT FOR SCHOOLS AND LIBRARIES.—

"(1) IN GENERAL.—In carrying out its responsibilities under subsection (h), each school or library to which subsection (h) applies shall—

"(A) adopt and implement an Internet safety policy that addresses—

"(i) access by minors to inappropriate matter on the Internet and World Wide Web;

"(ii) the safety and security of minors when using electronic mail, chat rooms, and other forms of direct electronic communications;

"(iii) unauthorized access, including so-called 'hacking', and other unlawful activities by minors online;

"(iv) unauthorized disclosure, use, and dissemination of personal identification information regarding minors; and

"(v) measures designed to restrict minors' access to materials harmful to minors; and

"(B) provide reasonable public notice and hold at least one public hearing or meeting to address the proposed Internet safety policy.

"(2) LOCAL DETERMINATION OF CONTENT.—A determination regarding what matter is inappropriate for minors shall be made by the school board, local educational agency, library, or other authority responsible for making the determination. No agency or instrumentality of the United States Government may—

"(A) establish criteria for making such determination;

"(B) review the determination made by the certifying school, school board, local educational agency, library, or other authority; or

"(C) consider the criteria employed by the certifying school, school board, local educational agency, library, or other authority in the administration of subsection (h)(1)(B).

"(3) AVAILABILITY FOR REVIEW.—Each Internet safety policy adopted under this subsection shall be made available to the Commission, upon request of the Commission, by the school, school board, local educational agency, library, or other authority responsible for adopting such Internet safety policy for purposes of the review of such Internet safety policy by the Commission.

"(4) EFFECTIVE DATE.—This subsection shall apply with respect to schools and libraries on or after the date that is 120 days after the date of the enactment of the Children's Internet Protection Act.".

SEC. 1733. IMPLEMENTING REGULATIONS.

Not later than 120 days after the date of enactment of this Act, the Federal Communications Commission shall prescribe regulations for purposes of section 254(l) of the Communications Act of 1934, as added by section 1732 of this Act.

SUBTITLE D—EXPEDITED REVIEW

SEC. 1741. EXPEDITED REVIEW.

(a) THREE-JUDGE DISTRICT COURT HEARING.—Notwithstanding any other provision of law, any civil action challenging the constitutionality, on its face, of this title or any amendment made by this title, or any provision thereof, shall be heard by a district court of 3 judges convened pursuant to the provisions of section 2284 of title 28, United States Code.

(b) APPELLATE REVIEW.—Notwithstanding any other provision of law, an interlocutory or final judgment, decree, or order of the court of 3 judges in an action under subsection (a) holding this title or an amendment made by this title, or any provision thereof, unconstitutional shall be reviewable as a matter of right by direct appeal to the Supreme Court. Any such appeal shall be filed not more than 20 days after entry of such judgment, decree, or order.

APPENDIX 17:
TABLE OF STATE CHILD PORNOGRAPHY STATUTES

STATE	STATUTE
Alabama	Code of Alabama, § 13-A-12-190, et seq.
Alaska	Alaska Statutes, § 11.41.455; 11.61.125
Arizona	Arizona Revised Statutes Annotated, § 13-3552, et seq.
Arkansas	Arkansas Statutes Annotated, § 41-4203, et seq.
California	California Penal Code, § 311.2, et seq.
Colorado	Colorado Revised Statutes, § 18-6-403, et seq.
Connecticut	Connecticut General Statutes Annotated, § 53a-196a; 196b
Delaware	Delaware Code Annotated, Title 11, § 1108
District of Columbia	District of Columbia Code, § 22-2011, et seq.
Florida	Florida Statutes Annotated, § 827.071
Georgia	Code of Georgia, § 26-9943a
Hawaii	Hawaii Revised Statutes, § 707-750; 751
Idaho	Idaho Labor Code, § 18-1507
Illinois	Illinois Revised Statutes, Chapter 38, § 11-20.1; § 3-6(c)
Indiana	Indiana Code Annotated, § 35-42-4-4
Iowa	Code of Iowa, § 728.12
Kansas	Kansas Statutes Annotated, § 21-3516
Kentucky	Kentucky Revised Statutes, § 531.300, et seq.
Louisiana	Louisiana Revised Statutes, § 14:81.1
Maine	Maine Revised Statutes Annotated, Title 17, § 2921, et seq.
Maryland	Maryland Annotated Code, Article 27, § 419A
Massachusetts	Massachusetts Annotated Laws, Chapter 272, § 29A, et seq.
Michigan	Michigan Statutes Annotated, § 750.145c

Minnesota	Minnesota Statutes Annotated, § 617.246, et seq.
Mississippi	Mississippi Code Annotated, § 97-5-31, et seq.
Missouri	Annotated Missouri Statutes, § 568.06, et seq.
Montana	Revised Montana Code Annotated, § 45-5-625
Nebraska	Nebraska Revised Statutes, § 28-1463, et seq.
New Hampshire	New Hampshire Revised Statutes Annotated, § 649-A
New Jersey	New Jersey Revised Statutes Annotated, § 2C:24-4
New Mexico	New Mexico Statutes Annotated, § 0-6A-1, et seq.
New York	New York Penal Law, § 263.00, et seq.
North Carolina	General Statutes of North Carolina, § 14.190.13, et seq.
North Dakota	North Dakota Century Code, § 12.1-27.2-01, et seq.
Ohio	Ohio Revised Code Annotated, § 2907.321, et seq.
Oklahoma	Oklahoma Statutes Annotated, Title 21, § 1021.2, et seq.
Oregon	Oregon Revised Statutes, § 163.483, et seq.
Pennsylvania	Pennsylvania Consolidated Statutes, Title 18, § 6312
Rhode Island	Rhode Island General Laws, § 11-9-1
South Carolina	South Carolina Code Annotated, § 22-22-22, et seq.
Tennessee	Tennessee Code Annotated, § 39-6-1137, et seq.
Texas	Texas Penal Code, § 43.25, et seq.
Utah	Utah Code Annotated, § 76-5a-1, et seq.
Vermont	Vermont Statutes Annotated, Title 13, § 2821, et seq.
Virginia	Code of Virginia Annotated, § 18.2-374.1
Washington	Washington Revised Code, § 9.68A.040, et seq.
West Virginia	West Virginia Code, § 161-8C-1, et seq.
Wisconsin	Wisconsin Statutes Annotated, § 940.203
Wyoming	Wyoming Statutes, § 6-4-403

APPENDIX 18:
STATE STATUTORY AGE FOR SEXUAL CONSENT

STATE	AGE
ALABAMA	16
ALASKA	16
ARIZONA	15
ARKANSAS	14
CALIFORNIA	18
COLORADO	18
CONNECTICUT	16
DELAWARE	16
DISTRICT OF COLUMBIA	16
FLORIDA	16
GEORGIA	16
HAWAII	16
IDAHO	18
ILLINOIS	17
INDIANA	16
IOWA	18
KANSAS	16
KENTUCKY	16
LOUISIANA	17
MAINE	16
MARYLAND	14
MASSACHUSETTS	16
MICHIGAN	16
MINNESOTA	16

STATE	AGE
MISSISSIPPI	16
MISSOURI	14
MONTANA	18
NEBRASKA	17
NEVADA	16
NEW HAMPSHIRE	16
NEW JERSEY	16
NEW MEXICO	18
NEW YORK	17
NORTH CAROLINA	16
NORTH DAKOTA	16
OHIO	16
OKLAHOMA	16
OREGON	18
PENNSYLVANIA	16
RHODE ISLAND	16
SOUTH CAROLINA	16
SOUTH DAKOTA	15
TENNESSEE	18
TEXAS	17
UTAH	14
VERMONT	16
VIRGINIA	13
WASHINGTON	18
WEST VIRGINIA	16
WISCONSIN	16
WYOMING	16

APPENDIX 19:
NON-PROFIT CHILD LOCATOR ORGANIZATIONS

STATE	ORGANIZATION	PHONE	FAX	EMAIL	WEBSITE
ARIZONA	The National Missing Children Organization, Inc.	800-690-FIND	602-944-7570	nmco-al@bham.net	http://www.nmco.org
ARKANSAS	Morgan Nick Foundation, Inc.	877-543-4673	501-632-0795	morgannick@aol.com	www.morgannick.com
CALIFORNIA	Child Quest International Inc.	408-287-HOPE	408-287-4676	info@childquest.org	http://www.childquest.org/
CONNECTICUT	The Paul and Lisa, Inc.	860-767-7660	860-767-3122	paulandlisaprogram @snet.net	http://www.paulandlisaorg/
FLORIDA	Child Watch of North America, Inc.	800-928-2445	407-876-4939	info@childwatch.org	www.childwatch.org

STATE	ORGANIZATION	PHONE	FAX	EMAIL	WEBSITE
KENTUCKY	Exploited Children's Help Organization	502-636-3670	502-636-3673	echolou@aol.com	http://www.echolou.org/prevention.php
MARYLAND	Missing and Exploited Children's Association	888-755-6322	410-296-7812	taavonjm@erols.com	http://www.mecaofmd.com
MICHIGAN	Missing Children's Network of Michigan	810-984-2911	none listed	mcnmi@i2k.com	http://www.i2k.com/~mcnmi/
MINNESOTA	Jacob Wetterling Foundation	800-325-HOPE	320-363-0473	jacob@uslink.net	www.jwf.org
MISSOURI	One Missing Link, Inc.	800-555-7037	417-886-9359	janismccall@hotmail.com	http://www.onemissinglink.org/omlindex.html
NEBRASKA	Missing Youth Foundation	402-289-4401	402-289-4626	info@missingyouth.com	http://www.discoveromaha.com/community/groups/missingyouth/
NEVADA	Nevada Child Seekers, Inc.	702-458-7009	702-451-4220	jill@nevadachildseekers.org	www.nevadachildseekers.org
NEW YORK	Child Find of America, Inc.	800-I-AM-LOST	914-255-5706	dlinder351@aol.com	www.childfindofamerica.org
OREGON	National Missing Children's Locate Center	800-999-7846	503-237-1443	nmclc@myexcel.com	http://www.findnv.org/

STATE	ORGANIZATION	PHONE	FAX	EMAIL	WEBSITE
PENNSYLVANIA	Children's Rights of Pennsylvania, Inc.	610-437-2971	none listed	none listed	none listed
TENNESSEE	Commission on Missing and Exploited Children (COMEC)	901-528-8441	901-575-8856	comec@netten.net	http://www.comec.org/
TEXAS	National Missing Children Center	800-832-3773	281-355-MISS	childsearch@childsearch.org	http://www.childsearch.org/
WASHINGTON	Operation Lookout/ National Center for Missing Youth	800-566-5688	425-348-4411	lookourfyi@operationlookout.org	www.operationlookout.org
WISCONSIN	Youth Educated in Safety, Inc.	800-272-7715	414-734-7077	yes3124@aol.com	http://www.yeswi.org
WYOMING	Christian Lamb Foundation	307-754-9261	307-754-4467	clamb@wavecom.net	www.clamb.org

APPENDIX 20:
STATE MISSING CHILDREN CLEARINGHOUSES

STATE	ORGANIZATION	WEBSITE	TELEPHONE
ALABAMA	Alabama Department of Public Safety, Missing Children Bureau	http://www.dps.state.al.us/public/abi/system/missing/children.asp	205-260-1100
ALASKA	Alaska State Troopers Missing Persons Clearinghouse	http://www.dps.state.ak.us/ast/abi/Bulletins.asp	800-478-9333
ARIZONA	Arizona Department of Public Safety, Criminal Investigation Research Unit	http://www.dps.state.az.us/agency/criminalinvestigations/intelligence/default.asp	602-223-2158
ARKANSAS	Arkansas Office of Attorney General, Missing Children Services Program	http://www.ag.state.ar.us/	501-682-1323

STATE	ORGANIZATION	WEBSITE	TELEPHONE
CALIFORNIA	California Department of Justice, Missing/Unidentified Persons	http://caag.state.ca.us/missing/index.htm	800-222-3463
COLORADO	Colorado Bureau of Investigation, Crime Information Center	http://www.cbi.state.co.us/mp/default.asp	303-239-4251
DELAWARE	Delaware State Police, State Bureau of Identification	http://www.state.de.us/missing/	302-739-5883
DISTRICT OF COLUMBIA	District of Columbia Metro Police Department, Missing Persons/Youth Division	none listed	202-576-6771
FLORIDA	Florida Department of Law Enforcement, Missing Children Information Clearinghouse	http://www.fdle.state.fl.us/missing_children/	800-342-0821
GEORGIA	Georgia Bureau of Investigation, Intelligence Unit	http://www.state.ga.us/gbi/	800-282-6564
HAWAII	Hawaii Department of the Attorney General, Missing Child Center	http://launch.hgea.org/HSC/	808 586-1449
IDAHO	Idaho State Police, Department of Criminal Investigation	http://www.isp.state.id.us/identification/sex_offender/	888-777-3922
ILLINOIS	Illinois State Police, I-SEARCH	http://www.isp.state.il.us/	800-843-5763
INDIANA	Indiana State Police, Indiana Missing Children Clearinghouse	none listed	800-831-8953
IOWA	Iowa Department of Public Safety, Division of Criminal Investigation	http://www.state.ia.us/government/dps/dci/mpic/index.htm	800-346-5507

STATE	ORGANIZATION	WEBSITE	TELEPHONE
LOUISIANA	Louisiana Department of Health and Human Services, Louisiana Clearinghouse for Missing and Exploited Children	none listed	504-342-4011
MAINE	Maine State Police, Criminal Investigation Division	http://www.maine.gov/dps/msp/criminal_investigation/cid_units.html	800-452-4664
MARYLAND	Maryland State Police, Maryland Center for Missing Children	http://www.inform.umd.edu/UMS+State/MD_Resources/MDSP/missingchild.html	800-637-5437
MASSACHUSETTS	Massachusetts State Police, Missing Persons Unit	http://www.state.ma.us/msp/missing.htm	800-622-5999
MINNESOTA	Minnesota State Clearinghouse, Bureau of Criminal Apprehension	http://www.dps.state.mn.us/bca/Invest/documents/Page-06.html	612-642-0610
MISSISSIPPI	Mississippi Highway Patrol	http://www.dps.state.ms.us/dps/dps.nsf/main?OpenForm	601-642-0610
MISSOURI	Missouri State Highway Patrol, Missing Persons Unit	http://www.mshp.dps.missouri.gov/MSHPWeb/Root/index.html	800-877-3452
MONTANA	Montana Department of Justice, Missing/Unidentified Persons	http://doj.state.mt.us/	406-444-3625
NEBRASKA	Nebraska State Patrol, Criminal Record and Identification Division	402-479-4019	
NEVADA	Nevada Office of the Attorney General, Missing Children Clearinghouse	http://ag.state.nv.us/menu/action_bttn/units/mcap/mcap.htm	702-486-3420
NEW HAMPSHIRE	New Hampshire State Police	http://www.nh.gov/safety/nhsp/mp.html	800-852-3411

STATE	ORGANIZATION	WEBSITE	TELEPHONE
NEW JERSEY	New Jersey State Police, Missing Persons/Child Exploitation	http://www.njsp.org/miss/mpu.html	800-743-5377
NEW MEXICO	New Mexico Department of Public Safety	http://missingpersons.osogrande.com/	505-827-9187
NEW YORK	New York Division of Criminal Justice, Service Missing and Exploited Children	http://criminaljustice.state.ny.us/missing/index.htm	800-346-3543
NORTH CAROLINA	North Carolina Center for Missing Persons, Crime Control and Public Safety	http://sbi.jus.state.nc.us/missing/missmain.htm	800-522-5437
NORTH DAKOTA	North Dakota Missing Children Clearinghouse	http://www.state.nd.us/radio/clearing.html	800-472-2121
OHIO	Ohio Office of the Attorney General, Missing Children Clearinghouse, Office of the Attorney General	http://www.mcc.ag.state.oh.us/	800-325-5604
OKLAHOMA	Oklahoma Office of the Attorney General, State Bureau of Investigation	http://www.oag.state.ok.us/oagweb.nsf/VServices!OpenPage	405-848-6724
OREGON	Oregon State Police, Missing Children Clearinghouse	http://egov.oregon.gov/OSP/MCC/child_index.shtml	800-282-7155
PENNSYLVANIA	Pennsylvania State Police, Bureau of Criminal Investigation	http://www.attorneygeneral.gov/theoffice.aspx?id=455	717-783-5524
RHODE ISLAND	Rhode Island State Police, Missing and Exploited Children	http://www.risp.state.ri.us/missingchildren/	401-444-1125

STATE	ORGANIZATION	WEBSITE	TELEPHONE
SOUTH CAROLINA	South Carolina Law Enforcement Division, Missing Persons Information Center	http://www.sled.state.sc.us/default.htm	800-322-4453
SOUTH DAKOTA	South Dakota Attorney General's Office, Division of Criminal Investigation	http://www.sddci.com/administration/missingpersons.htm	605-773-3331
TENNESSEE	Tennessee Bureau of Investigation, Criminal Intelligence Unit	http://www.ticic.state.tn.us/Missing_Children/miss_child.htm	615-741-0430
TEXAS	Texas Department of Public Safety, Criminal Intelligence Service	http://www.txdps.state.tx.us/mpch/	800-346-3243
UTAH	Utah Department of Public Safety, Bureau of Criminal Investigation	http://bci.utah.gov/MPC/MPCMissing.html	888-770-6477
VERMONT	Vermont State Police	http://www.dps.state.vt.us/vtsp/	802-773-9101
VIRGINIA	Virginia State Police, Department Missing Children's Clearinghouse	http://www.vsp.state.va.us/cjis_missing_children.htm	800-822-4453
WEST VIRGINIA	West Virginia State Police, Missing Children's Clearinghouse	http://www.wvstatepolice.com/children/children.shtml	800-352-0927
WASHINGTON	Washington State Patrol, Missing Children Clearinghouse	http://www.wa.gov/wsp/crime/mischild.htm	800-543-5678
WYOMING	Wyoming Office of the Attorney, General Division of Criminal Investigation	http://attorneygeneral.state.wy.us/dci/	307-777-7537

GLOSSARY

Abduction—The criminal or tortious act of taking and carrying away by force.

Abscond—To secrete oneself from the jurisdiction of the courts.

Acceptable use policy (AUP)—A set of guidelines and expectations about how individuals will conduct themselves online.

Adolescent—An individual older than 13 but younger than the age of majority or 18, whichever is smaller.

Acquiescence—Conduct that may imply consent.

Address—The unique location of an information site on the Internet, a specific file (for example, a Web page), or an email user.

Adult—An individual who has attained the age of majority.

Adult Verification Service—A service provided to businesses that validates the adult status of certain customers, e.g. by requiring a credit card.

Authentication—The process of confirming an asserted identity with a specified, or understood, level of confidence, such as a password.

Bandwidth—The amount of data that can be transmitted in a fixed amount of time. For digital devices, bandwidth is usually expressed in bits per second (bps) or bytes per second.

Binary—A number system that has just two unique digits.

Bit—Also referred to as a binary digit, it is the smallest element of computer storage.

Black List—In Internet filtering technology, refers to a list of websites, or URLs, to which access from a given workstation or user has been specifically forbidden.

Bookmark—A saved link to a website that has been added to a list of saved links so that you can simply click on it rather than having to re-type the address when visiting the site again.

Boolean Logic—A system of logic based on operators such as AND, OR, and NOT, in which search terms are linked with these Boolean operators to formulate more precise queries.

Broadband—A term used commonly to refer to communications or Web access that is faster than dial-up (56 k), including cable modems and digital subscriber lines.

Browser Software—The actual computer program used to view documents on the World Wide Web.

Bulletin Board—A computer system used as an information source and forum for a particular interest group

Byte—The common unit of computer storage, made up of eight bits (or binary digits), that holds the equivalent of a single character.

Cache—A place to store files locally for quicker access, e.g., memory and disk caches are used in every computer to speed up instruction execution and data retrieval.

CD-ROM—A computer disk that can store large amounts of information and is generally used on computers with CD-ROM drives.

CERT—The Computer Emergency Response Team based at Carnegie Mellon University.

Chat—Real-time conferencing between two or more users on the Internet. Chatting is usually accomplished by typing on the keyboard, not speaking, and each message is transmitted directly to the recipient.

Chat Room—A location on an online service that allows users to communicate with each other about an agreed-upon topic in real time—i.e., live—as opposed to delayed time as with email.

Child—Used to describe a broad category of individuals who are younger than adult.

Child Abuse—Any form of cruelty to a child's physical, moral or mental well-being.

Child Custody—The care, control and maintenance of a child which may be awarded by a court to one of the parents of the child.

Child Protective Agency—A state agency responsible for the investigation of child abuse and neglect reports.

Child Welfare—A generic term which embraces the totality of measures necessary for a child's well being; physical, moral and mental.

Click—A way of making a selection online.

Client—An application that runs on a personal computer or workstation and relies on a server to perform some operations.

Client-Side—Refers to any operation that is performed at the client workstation.

Content Provider—An organization or individual that creates information, educational, or entertainment content for the Internet.

Cookie—A message given to a Web browser by a Web server. The browser stores the message in a file and a message is then sent back to the server each time the browser requests a page from the server. Cookies are often used by websites to track users and their preferences.

Cost Per Acquisition (CPA)—An advertising model in which an advertiser pays a website operator for displaying an ad based on the number of new subscriptions the ad generates.

Cost Per Click (CPC)—An advertising model in which an advertiser pays a website operator a certain amount each time a user clicks on one of the advertiser's ads on the operator's website.

Cost Per Mille (CPM)—Refers to an advertising model in which an advertiser pays a website operator each time the advertiser's ad is displayed.

Cybersex—Online real-time dialog with someone—usually text-based—that interactively describes sexual behavior and actions with one's online partner for erotic purposes and expression.

Cyberspace—A term refers to the Internet or to the online or digital world in general.

CyberTipline—The program operated by the National Center for Missing and Exploited Children for reporting child abuse and child pornography.

Database—A collection of information organized in such a way that users can quickly select desired pieces of data.

Delinquent—An infant of not more than a specified age who has violated criminal laws or has engaged in disobedient, indecent or immoral conduct, and is in need of treatment, rehabilitation, or supervision.

Dial-up—The most common method for accessing the Internet. It involves making a connection from a user's computer—by using a modem—over a standard phone line to an Internet service provider.

Digital Subscriber Line (DSL)—A term used to denote a class of technologies that use copper phone lines to establish high-speed Internet connections between telephone switching stations and homes or businesses.

Domain Name Service (DNS)—An Internet service that translates domain names into IP addresses.

Download—The act of copying data from a main source to a peripheral device, e.g., copying a file from an online service to one's own computer.

Downward Departure—Refers to a situation where a court gives a defendant a sentence that is lesser than the one provided for in the Federal Sentencing Guidelines due to certain extenuating circumstances.

E-Mail—Also known as electronic mail, refers to a way of sending messages electronically from one computer to another, generally through a modem and telephone line connected to a computer.

Emancipation—The surrender of care, custody and earnings of a child, as well as renunciation of parental duties.

Encryption—Any procedure used in cryptography to convert plain text into cyphertext to prevent anyone but the intended recipient from reading the data.

File Attachment—A method by which users of e-mail can attach files to messages.

Filter—A type of technology that allows Internet material or activities that are deemed inappropriate to be blocked.

Freenet—A community network that provides free online access, usually to local residents, and often includes its own forums and news.

Graphics File—A file that holds an image, e.g., JPEG and GIF.

Hard Disk—A computer's primary storage medium, usually a fixed component within the computer itself.

Harvester—An automated program that is designed to collect e-mail addresses by scanning websites, bulletin boards, and chat rooms.

History File—The list most Web browsers maintain of downloaded pages in a session so that users can quickly review everything that has been retrieved.

Home Page—The site that is the starting point on the World Wide Web for a particular group or organization.

Hypertext Link—An easy method for retrieving information by choosing highlighted words or icons on the screen. The link will take you to related documents or sites.

Hypertext Markup Language (HTML)—The authoring language used to create documents on the Web.

Hypertext Transfer Protocol (HTTP)—A standard used by World Wide Web servers to provide rules for moving text, images, sound, video, and other multimedia files across the Internet.

Icon—A small picture on a Web page that represents the topic or information category of another Web page. Frequently, the icon is a hypertext link to that page.

In Loco Parentis—Latin for "in the place of a parent." Refers to an individual who assumes parental obligations and status without a formal, legal adoption.

ICQ ("I Seek You")—A conferencing program for the Internet that provides interactive chat and file transfer, and can alert users when someone on their predefined list is online.

ICRA—The Internet Content Rating Association.

Image Recognition—The process through which a computer can identify an image.

Incapacity—Incapacity is a defense to breach of contract which refers to a lack of legal, physical or intellectual power to enter into a contract.

Incest—The crime of sexual intercourse or cohabitation between a man and woman who are related to each other within the degrees wherein marriage is prohibited by law.

Infancy—The period prior to reaching the legal age of majority.

Infancy Presumption—At common law, the conclusive presumption that children under the age of seven were without criminal capacity.

Information Retrieval—The processes, methods, and procedures used to selectively recall recorded data from a database.

Instant Message (IM)—A two-way, real-time, private dialog between two users.

Intellectual Property—The ownership of ideas and control over the tangible or virtual representation of those ideas.

Internet—A worldwide collection of computer networks that allows people to find and use information and communicate with others.

Internet Protocol (IP)—A part of the TCP/IP suite of protocols that allows the various machines that make up the Internet to communicate with each other.

Internet Relay Chat (IRC)—An Internet conferencing system whereby the server broadcasts all messages to all current users of a particular channel.

Internet Service Provider (ISP)—An organization or company that provides access to the Internet, e.g., America Online.

Internet Telephony—Two-way transmission of audio over the Internet.

Instant Messages—Private, real-time text conversation between two users in a chat room.

IP Address—An identifier for a computer or device on a TCP/IP network.

Kidnapping—The illegal taking of a person against his or her will.

Link—Also known as a hyperlink, refers to a reference or pointer to another document.

Local Area Network (LAN)—A computer network that spans a relatively small area, e.g. a single building.

Log—A file that lists actions that have occurred.

Login—Also known as a user name, refers to the way that computers recognize users.

Megabyte (MB)—The term used to denote 1 million bytes.

Meta Tags—Elements within HTML code that allow page creators to describe the content of Web pages.

Metadata—A component of data which describes the content, quality, condition, or other characteristics of data.

Minor—A person who has not yet reached the statutory age of legal competence

Modem—A device that enables a computer to transmit digital data over analog telephone lines at different speeds, the highest of which transmits data the fastest.

Moderated NewsgroupA mailing list in which all postings are moderated by a specific individual with the authority and power to reject individual postings that he or she deems inappropriate.

Mouse—A small device attached to the computer by a cord, which lets you give commands to the computer. The mouse controls an arrow on the computer screen and allows you to point and click to make selections.

Mousetrapping—A technique that forces a user to remain on a specific website by not allowing the user to leave the site.

MPEG—A term that refers to the family of digital video compression standards and file formats developed by the Motion Picture Encoding Group, also often used to refer to the files of digital video and audio data available on the Internet.

Multimedia—Applications that combine text, graphics, full-motion video, and/or sound into an integrated package.

Napster—An application that gave individuals access to one another's music (MP3) files by creating a unique file-sharing system over the Internet.

Net—A short term for Internet.

Netiquette—Rules or manners for interacting courteously with others online, such as not typing a message in all capital letters, which is equivalent to shouting.

Newsgroup—An online discussion group.

Offline—The time that a user is not connected to the Internet.

Online—The time that a user is connected to the Internet.

Overblocking—Refers to a situation where Internet filtering software blocks access to resources that authorities did not intend to block.

Online Service—A company such as America Online or Prodigy that provides its members access to the Internet through its own special user interface as well as additional services such as chat rooms, children's areas, travel planning, and financial management.

Parens Patriae—Latin for "parent of his country." Refers to the role of the state as guardian of legally disabled individuals.

Password—A secret series of characters that enables a user to access a file, computer, or program.

Pixel—The smallest discrete element of an image or picture on a computer monitor, e.g. a single-colored dot.

Platform for Internet Content Selection (PICS)—A system for rating the content of websites that has been endorsed by the World Wide Web Consortium.

Plug-In—An auxiliary program, such as Windows Media Player, that works with Internet browser software to enhance its capability.

Portal—A website or service that offers a broad array of resources and services, such as e-mail, search engines, subject directories, and forums.

Precision—A measure of the effectiveness of information retrieval often expressed as the ratio of relevant documents to the total number of documents retrieved in response to a specific search.

Push Transfer—A form of data delivery in which data is automatically delivered to the user's computer without the user's having to make a request for the data.

Rape—The unlawful sexual intercourse with a person without his or her consent.

Real-Time Audio/Video—The communication of either sound or images over the Internet that occurs without delay in real time.

Recall—A measure of the effectiveness of document retrieval expressed as a ratio of the total number of relevant documents in a given database to the number of relevant entries or documents retrieved in response to a specific search.

Remote Viewing—The capability of system administrators to view what is being displayed on a given workstation or computer from their own location.

Scanner—A device that can copy text or illustrations printed on paper and translate that information into a form a computer can use.

Screen Name—A short nickname chosen by a computer user to employ when accessing his or her online service or network account.

Search Engine—A program that searches documents for specified words or phrases and returns a list of the documents where those items were found.

Server—A computer that delivers Web pages.

Server-Side refers—Any operation that is performed at the server.

Smart Card—A small physical hardware device containing read-only memory and a microprocessor that can be inserted into a card reader attached to a computer.

Software—A computer program or set of instructions. System software operates on the machine itself and is invisible to you. Application software allows you to carry out certain activities, such as word processing, games, and spreadsheets.

Spam—Refers to unsolicited e-mail, particularly unsolicited e-mail of a commercial nature.

Spider—A computer program that automatically retrieves Web documents.

Streaming Media—A technique for transferring data in such a way that it can be processed as a steady and continuous stream (as opposed to the user's needing to download the entire file before being able to view or listen to it).

Surfing—A metaphor for browsing the contents of the Web.

Teasers—Web pages or portions of websites that are intended to entice users to spend more time at a given website or become paying customers.

Thumbnail—A miniature display of a page or image.

Top-Level Domains—The major subdivisions within the Internet's domain name service (DNS).

Traffic—The number of visitors to a given website or resource.

Traffic Forwarding—The practice whereby one website forwards traffic to another website, often for a fee.

Transmission Control Protocol/Internet Protocol (TCP/IP)—The suite of communications protocols used to connect machines on the Internet. TCP/IP allows different hosts on the Internet to establish a connection with each other and exchange streams of data.

Underblocking—A situation whereby Internet filtering software does not block access to resources that authorities intended to block.

Uniform Resource Locator (URL)—The World Wide Web address of a site on the Internet.

Usenet—A worldwide bulletin board system that can be accessed through the Internet or through many online services, containing more than 14,000 forums, called newsgroups, that cover almost every imaginable interest group.

V-Chip—An electronic circuit or mechanism in a television that parents can use to block programs they consider inappropriate for their children. V-chips can be configured to block all programs of a given rating.

Virtual Hosting—The ability of Internet service providers or website operators to "host" websites or other services for different entities on one computer while giving the appearance that they exist on separate servers.

Virus—A piece of programming code inserted into other programming to cause some unexpected and usually undesirable event, such as lost or damaged files. Viruses can be transmitted by downloading programming from other sites or be present on a diskette. The source of the file you're downloading or of a diskette you've received is often unaware of the virus. The virus lies dormant until circumstances cause its code to be executed by the computer.

Web—A shortened form of World Wide Web (WWW).

Web Browser—A software program that lets you find, see, and hear material on the World Wide Web, including text, graphics, sound, and video. Popular browsers are Netscape, and AltaVista. Most online services have their own browsers.

Web Crawler—A computer program that automatically retrieves Web documents.

Web Page Hosting—The ability of Internet service providers, companies, or other organizations to act as a server of Web pages.

Webcam—A video camera that is used to capture periodic images or continuous frames to a website for display.

WebTV—A service that makes a connection to the Internet via a user's telephone service and then converts the downloaded Web pages to a format that can be displayed on a television.

Worldwide Web (WWW)—A hypertext-based system that allows you to browse through a variety of linked Internet resources organized by colorful, graphics-oriented home pages.

BIBLIOGRAPHY AND ADDITIONAL RESOURCES

Beyond Missing (Date Visited: May 2006) http://www.beyondmissing.com/.

Black's Law Dictionary, Fifth Edition. St. Paul, MN: West Publishing Company, 1979.

Carole Sund/Carrington Memorial Reward Foundation (Date Visited: May 2006) http://www.carolesundfoundation.com/

Federal Bureau of Investigation (Date Visited: May 2006) http://www.fbi.gov/.

KlaasKids Foundation (Date Visited: May 2006) http://www.klaaskids.org/.

National Center for Missing & Exploited Children (NCMEC) (Date Visited: May 2006) http://www.missingkids.com/.

National Crime Information Center (NCIC) (Date Visited: May 2006) http://www.fas.org/irp/agency/doj/fbi/is/ncic.htm/.

The National Runaway Switchboard (Date Visited: May 2006) http://www.1800runaway.org/.

Polly Klaas Foundation (Date Visited: May 2006) http://www.pollyklaas.org/.

Team H.O.P.E. (Date Visited: May 2006) http://www.teamhope.org/.

United States Department of Education (Date Visited: May 2006) http://www.ed.gov/.

United States Department of Justice, Office of Juvenile Justice and Delinquency Prevention (Date Visited: May 2006) http://ojjdp.ncjrs.org/.